MY WORLD ON AN ISLAND

GROWING UP IN BAR HARBOR

MY WORLD ON AN ISLAND

GROWING UP IN BAR HARBOR

Sylvia M. Kurson

Down East Books / Camden, Maine

Copyright © 1982 by Sylvia M. Kurson
ISBN 0-89272-126-X
Library of Congress Catalog Card Number 81-71562
Design: Lurelle Cheverie
Composition: Roxmont Graphics
Printed in the United States of America

DOWN EAST BOOKS / CAMDEN, MAINE 04843

Contents

Author's Note

Growing up in Bar Harbor in the years before the terrible 1947 fire was a movable feast. It was such a special place in those days: as green and blue and lovely, with its mountains rising out of the sea, as when the early French explorers first glimpsed it from their roving ships "and looked at each other with a wild surmise." It filled the eyes; it shook the senses; it was a truth beyond imagination.

Summers there were a living drama acted out by the fabled rich, with their chauffered limousines, their gymkhanas, and sailing races. We could watch the never-ending show and marvel, and watch and marvel we did. But while we looked on entranced, we knew that we could choose to leave the playhouse and step back happily into our own world where there was always something to do, something to see, something to feel that was ours alone.

The spring and fall and winter there belonged only to us. Perhaps that knowledge accounted in part for the intensity of our thinking, feeling, and doing. We used our world knowing that we could never use it all up.

I wrote this book because I longed to keep alive what it was like to grow up with Bar Harbor before the fire changed it forever, its beauty charred, its summer drama ended — before buses and planes and television made it only a part of the world outside.

In these fragments of life in my island world, I have used fictitious names whenever and wherever they would provide some degree of objectivity. Although the book is autobiographical, I wanted it to be less a concentration on me than a picture of a young girl's intense response to the beauty and variety of that enchanting island in that day.

Sylvia Kurson

Child in Maine Fog

In the white cocoon of fog
The bluebells   the wild roses
Are there in the warm salt air
High on the pink cliffs
Where they live.

When she wakes to the mourning foghorn
And sees outside her window
The blurred day,
She knows she will go down to the pink cliffs
To the bluebells   the wild roses
Fresh and clear in the salt mist
Sharp blue   soft white
Wet fragrance

She touches them with her eyes.

They are one in the fog
Closed in, alone together
Speaking a language unknown to the sun,
Fog whispering — fog dreaming
Secret   sweet
Now.

No Matter How
Hard You Try

I was four and a half, going on five, when I learned about grownups. You could do a big thing that made you cry because it mattered so much, and you knew you should be punished — but you weren't. You could do a little thing that didn't matter at all, and you didn't know why you were punished — but you were. I found out that to grownups big could be little, and little could be big.

That year of 1910 in Bar Harbor, Maine, we lived over my father's store, and Kucher's drugstore was right next door. Whenever I went by Kucher's, I used to push my nose against the window to see what they were showing that day. It was always worth looking at because of all the red and green and blue bottles. But one day the bottles were gone, and they had the biggest show I'd ever seen.

In the window was an old Indian man dressed up in leather with feathers on his head, and he was making rings out of blue-green stones! I watched him, keeping very still in case he should see me and stop doing this wonderful thing. Just then Mr. Kucher came into the window, put his hand on the Indian's arm, pointed to me, and said something. The Indian looked straight at me, his wrinkles all turning up into a smile, and motioned me to come in. I didn't know what to do, but he kept wagging his brown finger and smiling so I tiptoed in. He took me by the hand and led me over to his little pile of blue-green stones. "You like?" he asked. I just looked up at him and nodded hard. "Then I make you a ring, little girl, and it bring you good luck."

I watched him, holding my breath because I'd never seen anything like what his knobby brown hands were doing, stringing little blue beads on a kind of wire, then fitting the wire over my finger and twisting it shut.

"Now pretty little girl have pretty little ring," he said, patting me on the top of my head. "You keep."

I'd never been so happy in my whole life. My own Indian ring, made just for me! I couldn't wait to show it to my mother and tell her all about it.

She laughed when she saw it. "That's nice, dear," she said. "Did you remember to thank him?"

That afternoon I went down to the shore to play in the sand. I was alone. I liked being allowed to go by myself. Most days I dug a good-sized hole, filled it with beach stones, made a square sand hill over them, then wet the whole thing down with salt water. It was my very own castle; at least that's the way I saw it.

But that afternoon I had something different in mind. Instead of burying beach stones, I'd bury my ring, pile the sand over it, sit back and make up a story. The story would tell of a little princess who buried her very best treasure just so she could shiver with fear that it was lost forever — but she'd shiver only long enough to feel the fear wearing out. Then she'd dig around the castle wall little by little, kind of licking at it the way you do an ice-cream cone. She'd dig around until she couldn't hold back any longer, and the moment had come to scrabble wildly into the mound for her buried treasure, find it just where she'd put it, wash off the sand in her bucket of water, and become the only little princess in the whole wide world who'd rescued an Indian ring of blue stones made just for her.

The play went off exactly the way I'd planned, except that I took extra time to look at my empty ring finger, feel sorry for it, and see in my mind the nice old Indian man shaking his brown finger at me for burying his beautiful present.

I'd been so busy with my digging and burying and dreaming that I'd lost track of real time. The tide was coming in. The sand beneath me was turning dark, and my bare feet were beginning to feel damp-cold.

"Oh, you musn't come up yet!" I yelled at the tide. "My ring, my ring, give me time to get back my ring!"

I jumped up from where I'd been kneeling, grabbed my shovel, and tore into the mound. The sand was wet-heavy now. It came up in slices. I threw slice after slice to the side. I dug with the shovel and then with my hands, faster and faster, but I could feel the tide sucking the sand down under my fingers and the water coming back up. Then there was nothing but black mud, and I knew at last that my beautiful ring was gone forever.

I climbed the hill to home, stumbling and crying. I'd lost the very best thing I'd ever had. And how was I going to tell my mother? What would she do to me? Once, in the middle of the night, my parents had got my brothers and me up and dressed, telling us we might have to leave because the hotel across the street was on fire. We all huddled together in the front window watching the flames shooting up in the sky and the firemen running back and forth with hoses, aiming them wherever new flames started up. I'd been frightened then, but *I* hadn't started the fire, and it wasn't *my* home that was burning down. This was much worse because *I* was the one who had dug the hole, and *I* was the one who had lost my ring!

My mother looked scared when I dragged myself into the parlor, covered with muddy sand and crying so hard I had the hiccoughs.

"Why, what in the world has happened to you?" she

asked, putting out her arms for me to go to her. But I couldn't. I'd have to tell her first, and then she wouldn't want to hug me.

I told her the whole story. It took a long time because I was so scared and sobbing so hard. Then I just stood there, shaking and waiting.

"Oh, for heaven's sake!" she said, letting her breath out. "Is that all? I thought you'd gotten yourself into real trouble. Wipe up now, and you can take some of my fresh-baked cookies. Come on. It's all over now."

I took the cookies. But it wasn't all over for me, and it never would be.

Another day something else happened. I'd been over at Janey's, skipping rope and swinging on her swing, and we'd been getting ready to play Haley Over when her mother called her in. It was too early for me to go home, but ever since I'd lost my ring I didn't want to do anything by myself, so home I went and wished I hadn't.

I'd forgotten that my mother was having a whist party that afternoon and didn't want me getting in the way. Mama and I had fun together most of the time, but not on party days, when she'd fly off the handle at all of us. Papa couldn't ride me around on his back for fear of mussing up the parlor rug. And Maud, our hired girl, wouldn't talk to me; she'd be too mad at Mama for making her do extra cleaning.

"You be a good girl when the ladies come," Mama said. "Now go wash your hands and face and get behind your ears. Is your dress fit to be seen?" She looked me over front and back. "It'll do, I guess, if you stay out of mischief. I'm going to get dressed now. You look at your picture books and don't bother Maud. She'll eat your head off if you make any mess."

When I'd done what I was told to do — except that I kind of dabbed around with the washcloth and skipped my ears — I was hungry, so I went out to the kitchen. The floor had been scrubbed up and the stove blacked. Everything had been put away except the party plates on the dresser with the party treats laid out on them. They looked good. I wanted some so I took several Meribel cookies, the kind Mama always made for parties. I was just going back to my room when Mama came in. She looked pretty with her hair done up high over her forehead. She smelled pretty, too — that nice, cool mayflower smell she always put on when she got dressed up.

"Well," she said, "I guess we're about ready." She was looking at me with a faraway look, as if I was just something else in the kitchen. "Now you be sure . . ." Suddenly she stared straight at me. "Julie, you're eating. What . . . Oh, no, you didn't!" Her eyes darted over to the party plates, and she saw the holes where the cookies used to be. "Julie, I've told you and told you . . ." She was shaking her head from side to side, and the blue in her eyes looked almost black. "I had those plates set out with the thinnest and best-shaped cookies. You've been a naughty girl, and I'll have to punish you. Come here."

I didn't move. I couldn't. She seemed to be swelling up, getting bigger and bigger while I was getting littler and littler.

Then she was spanking me on the palm of my hand, and I was crying. The spanking didn't hurt. I was crying because Mama was mad at me about cookies. I'd lost my beautiful Indian ring, and she wasn't mad. She'd even told me to take some cookies. This time I'd taken cookies, and she was mad enough to spank me. I was all mixed up.

But I learned about grownups in those days. I learned that no matter how hard you try, you can't figure them out — ever.

For Fred

I wonder if anyone else remembers Fred Lederer, and if so, how they picture him. As a disreputable old drunkard? As a crazy old man who had a penny-candy store in his shack down at the foot of School Street? As that old German who couldn't speak English and came under suspicion during the war? Or do they remember him as I do — with a strange kind of love. For it was Fred Lederer — or Fred Leatherhead as we kids always called him — who brought mystery and drama into our lives.

Our red-letter days were Fred Leatherhead days when at least one of our bunch had a begged or earned penny or two to spend. Whoever the lucky one was, he or she passed the word along to the others on an elaborately folded and refolded scrap of paper smuggled around behind the teacher's back. All it ever said was "Fred." That was enough. The message was clear. The minute school let out we were making a beeline for Fred and his excitingly unpredictable world in that two-room shack down on School Street.

"Hope he's drunk," one of us always said, because when he was, he'd stumble down the small closed-in stairway from the room upstairs, groaning and swearing, and grope his way over to the candy case. When we'd pointed to what we wanted, he'd groan some more and give us twice as much candy as we were supposed to get for a penny.

Our choice was always the same — Baked Beans, the little red balls with Spanish peanuts inside.

If he used his measuring cup, as he did on the rare days when he was sober, we'd get what you'd get at Lufkin's or Green's or anywhere else, just ten to twelve for a penny.

But one day when he was so drunk that he staggered and almost fell into the glass case, he heaved the cup across the room, roared like a maddened bull, shoveled up a huge handful in his great paw, and filled the striped candy bag so full he couldn't twist it shut.

One of us grabbed it fast, said, "Thanks, Mr. Lederer," and hot-footed it out the door with the rest of us in close pursuit. Outside we counted our loot. Fifty-three Baked Beans! That was a record never surpassed.

But it wasn't just the dark and smelly cave of a shack, the groaning and swearing, and the Baked Beans that pulled us into his world. Fred was something wonderful to see. He was a mountain of a man, almost as big around as he was tall. His black hair stood up from his forehead like a wire brush. His big black mustache, which spread almost from ear to ear, turned down like the arms of a horseshoe. Between groans he muttered thickly in a foreign language, always angrily, always fighting an invisible enemy. We couldn't understand a word of what he was saying, but that was all to the good. Half-giggling, half-scared, and wholly caught up in the dark drama, we could imagine the most deliciously horrible worst.

Old Fred Leatherhead! We liked to wonder about him, talk about him, be afraid of him. Best of all, we liked to pass over from our own too well-regulated world into his thrillingly crazy kingdom where no one ever had to dust or wash, where swearing wouldn't bring on the threat of having your mouth washed out with soap, where a dark giant staggered across the shack-floor stage, where drunkenness promised a Baked Bean bonanza.

I don't know why the ghost of Fred Lederer keeps coming back to haunt me. Is he asking to be seen as he maybe really was, not as we made him up to be? After all, nobody knew why he groaned and drank and was always fighting an invisible enemy. Sickness? Loneliness? The prison of a language barrier?

I'll never know. But whatever the answer, he deserves to be remembered for lighting up our afternoons in that wonderful dark world down on School Street.

'Tis a Bond

In Sarah Orne Jewett's "The Queen's Twin," Abbie Martin in downeast Maine thinks of herself as Queen Victoria's twin because they were born on the same day, at exactly the same hour, in the same year. "Say what you may," Mrs. Martin tells her visitors, "'tis a bond between us."

Now, no such coincidental bond exists between novelist Louis Auchincloss and me, but I claim kinship nevertheless — a kinship dating from the day when I was permitted to step foot into the Auchincloss "cottage" in Bar Harbor. In the cellar of that house I broke bread with his caretaker-gardener, and through that house I raced at will one never-to-be-forgotten winter Saturday. Are stronger elements needed for a presumptive bond?

It all came about quite naturally. Brick Bragdon was my next-door neighbor and what-are-we-going-to-do-today friend. Her father was caretaker for the Auchincloss estate. Every morning except Sunday, he tramped the three miles from his house to his job, spent the day seeing to whatever needed doing inside or outside the cottage, then tramped the three miles home in time for supper. When the notion was put to him that he might take Brick and me along with him one Saturday, he reared up and balked. But Brick went at him with all her only-daughter blandishments, and when his good wife let fire with "Now Henry, you get her out from under my feet for one blessed day!" he succumbed, shaking his head dolefully at the prospect.

And so we packed up our vittles in an oilcloth bag and went forth like a tandem of squaws following an unwilling brave.

Three miles is no slouch of a hike for anyone on a Maine winter day with the thermometer down to zero, but dressed in tassled caps, woolly coats, two layers of mittens, and felt-lined overshoes, we took the distance as easily as animals bound for prey. The adventure of what lay ahead of us kept us hot on the heels of our reluctant leader.

From time to time he'd stop in his tracks, turn his head around to see how we were doing, grunt, and go on. He was not given to wasting words, and certainly wasn't spending any on us that day.

The Auchincloss cottage looked like a fairy castle in the snow, ivory white against blue white, framed in the dark of firs. Whether it was as beautiful as I remember it, I don't know, and it doesn't matter. What we saw seemed a palace to two ten-year-olds conditioned to stand in awe of summer visitors' wealth and rich possessions. To enter that palace even through the cellar door was to enter another world where magnificent people lived magnificent lives beyond our wildest imaginings.

We stamped the snow off our overshoes. Brick's father policed the operation, grunted eventual satisfaction, unlocked the door, and led the way into a basement room as big as the town roller-skating rink. There was little to see: a tall woodstove with an outsized pot belly, a jumble of flower pots and flat boxes, one kitchen chair with a sagging cane bottom, and mounds of raffia piled up around it. But to our bemused eyes, it was a place arrayed in mysterious splendor.

The silence was overwhelming. We hardly dared breathe for fear of starting an echo to disturb it.

Brick's father went about his business at once. He chunked the stove, put a match to it, finished the match on his corncob pipe, and settled into the chair. "Now you young'uns stay put over there," he said, pointing to a piece of the wall and floor just within reach of where he was sitting, "and behave yourselves. There's work to be done, and I aim to do it."

We sat on the cement floor, backs against the wall, so caught up in the wonder of where we were that we didn't know we were cold until the fire took hold and thin heat crept toward our toes. Then we began to smell cold getting warm, dry bulb dirt, and the corncob pipe. We shifted our bottoms and let out our breaths. We were beginning to feel at home in the palace.

Mr. Bragdon worked. We watched and marveled at the easy way he was doing queer things with the raffia, almost as if he was puttering with tangled fish lines in his own woodshed.

Because the winter days were short, he was ready early for the lunch he'd brought in a lard pail. He had one of his own home-cured stripped fish, some soda biscuits, and a quart jar of stewed tea. We'd brought sugar doughnuts, molasses cookies, and apples — a feast more exotic in that setting than jellied eels and escargots. To this day I can taste the smoky saltiness of the stripped fish and the brown sweetness of that stewed tea.

That would have been a great plenty of goodness, but there was more to come. Almost before the last crumb had been disposed of, Mr. Bragdon's eyelids began to go up and down with a jerky motion. Brick poked me with her elbow, a signal I recognized immediately as a prepare-for-action alert, and I gathered myself together, ready to spring.

When the eyelids stopped going up, and long puffing noises came from behind the bushy mustache, we started stirring, a little at a time — one leg, then another, then both. A moment's wait to be sure of safety. A final decisive jab, and we were off on a wild voyage of discovery up the cellar stairs, through the door at the top, into a kitchen bigger than the whole ground floor of Brick's house or mine.

"Look at that, would you! And that! And that!"

But there was no time for loitering. We raced madly through two dining rooms, three sitting rooms, room after room of sheet-covered furniture, our breaths leaving wakes of mist behind us. If there'd been time to realize what we were seeing, we might have felt some uneasiness about being where we had no business to be — it was all so quietly private, so smug against invasion, so invested with the strangeness of difference.

But time was running out, and there was too much left to explore. Without the exchange of a single spoken word, we knew what we meant to do — go through every last room in the whole house. Unless we did, we'd never be sure we hadn't missed the only other eye-popping revelation.

So on we raced, up another flight of stairs, through enormous bedrooms and baths, up to the top floor where the rooms dwindled in size and looked more like our own.

In the last room we were brought up short. The moment had come to turn back, but in that moment Brick's eyes fastened on a stray coat-hanger lying on an iron bed. Should we? She looked at me for affirmation.

"Too big. It'd stick out of your coat."

Her face crumpled. Then she nodded slowly, recognizing sad truth for what it was. We would have to leave empty-handed with no booty-proof to show off to our friends.

Back to the cellar was downstairs all the way. We made it with moments to spare. When Brick's father woke up, we were sitting like the good children he'd told us to be, backs against the wall, legs stretched out straight on the floor, waiting demurely for further orders.

"You young'uns about ready to call it a day?" He sounded relieved that the sky hadn't fallen in, and less disposed to expect the worst.

"If *you* are, Daddy," Brick said so sweetly she should have gagged.

"Well now, you've had you quite a day I'd say," and something like a smile flicked across his face.

We had, all right — more of a day than he could ever suspect.

There Was Always Something to Do

There was always something to do, something to see down on the shore, up on the mountains, deep in the woods. Starfish and sea anemones sheltered in the brack of the tide pools. Soldier moss, painted trillium, jack-in-the-pulpit grew in the light-spattered dark of the forests.

We popped the pods of seaweed, our free balloons — snap, squish. And we took turns skimming stones out into the harbor: two skips, five, once even nine. On that day we played Follow the Leader in the wake of the winner and skinned our knees and scraped our shins and laughed when they hurt. "It's nothing," we said, and it *was* nothing, nowhere near so important as Skipping Nine Times.

And once, somewhere between the ocean and the mountains, where sun never reached over the thick overhang of branches, we found clay, and to us it was gold. We dug fast and hard in the rich goo with a rusty can torn down one side, and we filled it and bore it home rejoicing.

Brothers' eyes lighted up, seeing stupendous possibilities.

"Where?"

"Shan't tell."

"Give you a penny. A fishline? Five cigar rings?"
"No."
"Get some for us?"
"Why?"
"Want it for something."
"What?"
"You get it and see."

Always we wanted to see, so the next day we went back to the pit, this time with a lard pail and a spoon for digging.

They grabbed for the pail.

"Hey, now you going to tell us?"

They looked at each other, and some sign must have passed between them. "Girls!" one said, and the tone was not admiring, but it meant, Yes.

That was Act One, Scene One, in a drama that caught us up in its headlong rush toward disaster.

There were things to do, and it appeared that, girls though we were, we were to play some essential roles. The plot centered around our clay gold, which was to be transfigured by our alchemy into playing marbles. The brothers had fallen on hard times. The beanbag, once stuffed to capacity with store-bought marbles, had lost too much weight, and their exchequer was in like condition. Recouping had looked impossible—until now.

They had planned the work detail like chain-gang bosses. On the assembly line down in the basement, one scooped out with his fingers bits of clay to shape into rough balls; the other molded them smooth. That done to satisfaction, the balls came over to us for baking in the furnace — a process fraught with peril to our hands and the marbles-to-be, which had a sneaky way of rolling off the cookie sheet into the coals. We lost a goodly number. The boys uttered bitter words. We improved. We had to. It was that or be fired.

When the baked balls had cooled off enough to handle, it was our privilege to paint them, mostly blue. We'd used up too much of the other colors in our Prang water-color set on our paper dolls. The boys had more to say about that.

It was suppertime when we finished laying out the last marbles on taken-apart brown-paper bags.

The boys stretched tall and gloated. We took pains to stay off center stage lest they pull the curtain on us. Act Three had been scheduled to be played on our sidewalk after school the next day, and although our status would shift from actors to audience, we *had* to be there. After all, we'd discovered the clay gold. We'd baked and painted the marbles. It was no more than our due to be in on the grand climax.

As it turned out, we were the only audience for the shoot-out. The boys had been careful to play down the con-frontation. It was to be just an everyday rolling.

We watched from the balcony (which was only our front porch on lesser occasions). And we kept our mouths shut as we'd been ordered to do on pain of explicitly defined horrible retribution should we transgress.

The battle plan had been brilliantly conceived. In Game One both contending forces used equal ammunition, orthodox store-bought marbles, the boys having shaken the last sad few from the emaciated beanbag.

It was two wins to one for the opposition in the first round, which lasted so long that we began to entertain the idea of taking time out for refreshments.

Then suddenly the moment we'd been waiting for burst upon us. The brothers began shooting with our home-grown missiles.

There was a quick flash of blue. The ball split. Another, and it crumbled. The third slewed off the course and decapitated itself against the hose spigot on the side of the house. The play was over. It had ended ignominiously.

The opposition went mad with derisive joy. The brothers shrank down into themselves until they looked so reduced that we had to stop looking. There'd been times when we would have welcomed even the weakest stroke of rough justice, but this was not one of them. We were on their side. We'd trained in a hard school for this moment. It was a defeat for them and us and our clay gold.

But life with the brothers had taught us to take our losses philosophically if we were to survive, so we slipped into the house and homed in on the cookie jar.

Between munchings we discussed with remarkable calm the options for tomorrow.

There was always something to do, something to see.

Once Upon a Fourth

Fourth of July in a Maine village before World War I was justly celebrated — at least by the kids who grew up in the latter days of what writers call the Age of Innocence.

Lay hands on enough wealth to buy firecrackers, cap pistols, or, if your folks wouldn't trust you with anything more interesting, the lowly sparklers. Roam around town with all the other roamers. Get in on a political rally if the politician was throwing out pennies for a scramble. Shove your way onto the free visitors' launch out to whatever battleship was anchored in the harbor. All these things were exciting to have and to do — but they were not in the same league with what my brothers had in mind on the particular Fourth I'm remembering.

I'd heard them plotting in their bedroom at night.

"Ma'll never let us do it."

"Yeah. But what if we just do it without asking?"

There was a sizeable silence while they pondered. I figured that Older Brother was recollecting how Ma had hit the ceiling when he wanted to get into long pants and raised the roof when he wanted to go out for football.

"I dunno. It'd take a lot of hard living after."

"Say, why don't *you* ask her?" Older Brother had his ways of achieving his ends. "She's easier on you."

"Tell you what . . ." Younger Brother had observed Older Brother's frontal attacks and their consequences often enough to know that for any success at all you had to approach the enemy from the side when she was off-guard cleaning house or cooking for a party. "She's having her whist gang on Monday — Shrimp Wiggle and all that junk. I'll try her out when she's up to her elbows in dough."

"Yeah. She don't hear too good when she's flummoxing around on some new upside-down cake to put Lizzie Connors' nose out of joint."

Whist Party Day arrived. The house shook with preparations. We got slim pickings with leftovers at noon. Ma likely would have skipped the meal entirely if she could have got away with it, but she knew she had to feed us before she could get us out from underfoot.

"Say, Ma," Younger Brother was pitching his voice kind of soft and even. No emphasis. Just casual sweet reasonableness. "It's the Fourth next Tuesday and the fellers are doing something a little different this year—getting in on the beginning and staying through to the end."

Ma was off somewhere. If she heard voices, they came through from too far away to bother with at the moment.

"Yes, dear. Now where do you think Aunt Flo's embroidered runner's got to . . ."

"Dave and John and Carlyle and the rest of the crowd are planning to celebrate our country's independence by staying out all night. We kind of thought . . ."

It was an awful mistake — like hollering at someone deaf and having them roar back at you, "You don't have to burst my eardrums!"

She reared back and let him have it, both barrels. *"Stay out all night?"* Well, I should just say you've got another think coming, Mister Man! You'll do no such thing. You'll be back in this house by curfew time, and that's all about it!"

The next days were a long sight worse than Whist Party Day. Nobody did much talking. Ma had her buttoned-up mouth on her. The boys said, "Yes, Ma'am," "No, Ma'am," and nothing else.

It took Pa to break the deadlock. To this day we don't know what ammunition he used, but he must have nicked her just hard enough to straighten her out. *The boys could stay out all night.*

The Fourth was the Fourth with its usual catastrophes. Somebody's cap pistol blew off a fingernail. Firecrackers smouldered out without going off. The launches to the battleship stopped running early in the day when the crowds got too big to handle.

But the boys stayed out all night, and I stayed awake till 10:30, when I heard Ma and Pa tiptoe downstairs to reconnoiter the territory outside. I crept down in their wake, not knowing what I hoped they'd discover. It was late for me, who was too young to be up after nine, and I was wildly happy with the strangeness.

They inched open the front door a crack, stuck their heads around the opening, and peered out. Then they did the last thing I would have expected. They looked at each other and laughed! I laughed, too, for company, but it wasn't until I saw what they had seen that I knew why they were laughing.

There on the porch swing were the boys, packed head to feet like sardines, sleeping the sleep of the just.

Ma and Pa left them there all night. They must have done some shivering because a cold sea fog had come up early in the evening. But they'd got their wish. They'd celebrated the Fourth by staying out all night.

Town Meeting

That town meeting in the teens of the twentieth century came perilously close to splitting Bar Harbor down the middle.

The lines had been drawn as soon as word got around, and it got around as fast as fire in high wind.

"Meddlin' busybodies out to do away with our own band concerts in the village green and put a piece of the Boston Symphony into the bandstand where it don't belong and never will!"

"No fools like old fools for not moving with the times. Sure, our band's all right for winter, but summer's another story. The rusticators want better, and they're going to get it!"

"Over our dead bodies!"

The issue was shaping up for civil war with nothing civil about it. Carnage was expected at town meeting.

The grammar school's principal had the notion that crucial history was in the making; he let us all out to go to the Casino, where we would see it made in true Yankee fashion.

I doubt that many of us cared much one way or another, except that getting out of school was always cause for rejoicing. Who played the concerts that lured us to the village green in the evenings was generally of little matter. Under cover of darkness and "The Stars and Stripes Forever," or "The Anvil Chorus," or anything loud enough to keep us safe, we could and did commit mindless and comparatively innocent mayhem.

But that day we could see that trouble was brewing all over the Casino. The place was packed. There was a groundswell of muttering. The moderator would have his hands full calling for order and sweet reason.

I'd never laid eyes on half the people there. They must have come out of the back of beyond to see the show and to do battle if need be. In their winter duds — earlap caps and mackinaws and high laced boots — they looked fully equipped to weather whatever storms might come. I was puzzled. Why should they care who played for the village green band concerts?

The air was thickening. People were hot and mad, ready for action.

At last it was time. The gavel came down with authority. But before the moderator could open his mouth and the meeting begin, an old man in the front row was up on his feet and going nonstop.

"About this here Boston Symphony idee. I don't know who's behind it, but I know I ain't, not by a long sight and in no manner at all."

The muttering swelled to a bass roar with a heavy drumbeat of clapping.

A voice from the balcony bellowed, "Sit down up front! Hold up. You're out of order."

"Don't care if I am. I'll speak my piece here and now." And he did. The Boston Symphony should be told to stay home where they belonged.

The moderator pounded frantically.

The meeting roared him down.

The battle was engaged.

"We want our own band. They look good and they sound good and they're ours!"

"How in God's name can you compare the two? Anyone in his right mind should jump at the chance to get the Boston Symphony. It's class!"

"Yeah, but can they play as loud?"

"Oh hell, if it's noise you want . . .!"

The war of nerves was turning into a war of attrition with no end in sight.

It took a matron of the Eastern Stars to arbitrate. "Mr. Moderator, with all due respect, I want to put a fair motion. I move that we have our own band play four nights a week. The Boston Symphony can have the three nights in between. That way we show we stand by our own and still give the Symphony their chance."

She was a sparrow of a woman, but her eyes and her voice were strong with conviction. And she was making sense — the most valued commodity in Yankee reasoning.

They didn't rise up and call her blessed, but the muttering died down to murmuring, and for the first time that day, the voice of the gavel was heard in the land.

The motion was entertained, seconded, and put to a vote. The article passed. Once again town-meeting democracy had prevailed.

The French Incident

All of this curious tale happened in a downeast island village in 1919.

We kids had been called a raft of names including "them rips of Satan" for smuggling some ripe stripped fish into the cloakroom at school and "them ornery little bastids" for doing no more than helping the boys relocate an outhouse or two on Halloween. But until Marguerite Connors called us "mes petits choux," we'd never so much as blinked an eyelash. After all, as someone else said, "What's in a name?"

We'd just wound up a session of making Maybaskets over at Pauline's house. The finished products looked pretty sick and tired by the time we'd messed through the cutting and pasting and crimping, but Pauline had revived our spirits with sardines and crackers. Sure, we were liberally anointed with flour paste and fish oil — all except Marguerite, who always managed to stay "sweet and pretty" — but as we saw it, she had no business to be calling us names we couldn't understand.

She'd just stood there on the corner of her street, smirking at us the way she always did when we got ourselves into a mess she'd steered clear of, and said in a put-on drawl, "Goodnight, mes petits choux. Maybe we can get together tomorrow," and off she went, swinging her prissy bottom.

"What was that she called us?" Jessie said, her eyes narrowed into slits, her teeth bared as if ready to bite.

"I didn't get it, but I didn't like it," I said, kicking a pebble into the nearest telephone post. 'May petty chew' was all I could make out of it, but whatever it was, if she thinks she can get away with it, she's got another think coming!"

This mes-petits-choux thing had set off a fuse that was ready to go anyway. A while ago, three of our bunch had been kicked out of the library for rustling candy bags. Not long after, Marguerite had bestowed upon her by the same librarian a book of fairy tales for being "the best behaved young lady to come into the library." She'd rubbed our noses in it, figuratively speaking, but we couldn't go at her openly without showing our hands to our mothers, who were forever holding her up to us as what none of us was: "a nice little girl who stays out of mischief."

And besides that, she was everlastingly bragging about how her mother got to be a secretary for one of the summer people because she "can speak French." She didn't come right out and say, "Your mothers can't," but we got the message, and it was not sweet to our ears.

The next time she called us whatever that outlandish thing was, we backed her up against the gym wall. "Now that's enough," Barbara said, spacing out the words to give them time to sink in. Barb had been with us the other time, but she was slower to boil over and never said much, anyway. "You just say flat out what you mean and say it in plain English, or you can stand there the rest of your days."

At first Marguerite made out to look surprised. Then she smiled brightly. "Oh, didn't you know? But of course you wouldn't. It's French. It means 'my little cabbages,' and my mother says it's a term of endearment."

I looked at Jessie, who was looking at Barbara, who was looking at me. We'd been tipped off balance. How can you tackle somene who's calling you a term of endearment? We knew she was doing it to get to us, but we couldn't prove it. And how can you get mad about a foreign language because you can't speak it?

"Well," Jessie said pretty weakly for her, "we don't care to be called cabbages. We're not, and it's silly. So don't do it again, or we'll trim your sails good."

The third time came a week later just before homeroom period. Marguerite had waited until the bell was due to ring. "See you later, mes petits choux," she threw over her shoulder as she steered for safety.

The teacher didn't get much value out of Jess and Barb and me during first period, and that was unusual because we liked Miss Johnson, and English was our favorite subject. She was having us read aloud, a farm story that wasn't all prettied up and made good sense. When we were called on, we did our job, but just barely.

Miss Johnson was looking put out. "I don't know what's got into some of you people this morning, but perhaps we can get a decent reading out of Marguerite. Do you feel up to it, Marguerite?" she asked, sounding pretty fed up.

"Oh yes, Miss Johnson. There's nothing wrong with *me*," she said, looking sweet enough to make you gag.

"Well, I'm certainly glad to hear that. Read, please, and the rest of you pay attention."

Marguerite began at a great rate, giving the farm story more fancy dramatics than I imagine the writer intended, and we'd tuned her out when a sudden silence jerked us out of our deep-sea depression.

"Please read the last sentence again, Marguerite."

Marguerite looked puzzled. "Is something wrong, Miss Johnson?"

"Just read it again, please."

We snapped to attention, sitting up as stiff and

straight as if yanked by invisible wires. If something was wrong, we weren't about to miss it.

Marguerite read the sentence again. "Eben thrust his fork deep into the pile of manuray."

There was a second of absolute silence before the class began to whoop and holler. Just plain old horse manure, and Marguerite, who was too nasty-nice dainty to have any truck with the earthier words in the English language, was calling it "manuray"!

When Miss Johnson, who was having some trouble straightening out her own face, had finally settled us down, she spoke to Marguerite gently. "The word you mispronounced is manure, Marguerite. It means animal dung, and Eben was forking it for fertilizer."

"Of course I knew that, Miss Johnson," Marguerite said snippily, but her face was redder than we'd ever seen it, "but it isn't a very nice word and I thought it would sound nicer if I gave it the French pronunciation."

Miss Johnson got straight to the point. "The word is manure, Marguerite, a good honest English word. From now on you will read what's written without trying to fix it up to suit your own taste. Class dismissed."

We were waiting for her out in the hall. "Had enough French, Marguerite?" Jessie asked, her grin wide enough to split her face.

Marguerite glared at us. "Oh you, you're all impossible!" and she swished away.

But from that day on we heard no more of "mes petits choux."

The Court Martial

There was trouble that Monday of May 1919, in Bar Harbor, Maine, and the girls were right smack in the middle of it.

We called ourselves "our bunch" and ran around together, getting along about as well as any eleven-year-olds do — getting mad at each other, making up, getting into trouble, wriggling our way out, but this time the trouble was different — bigger — and so far there didn't seem to be any way out.

It had happened the Saturday before at Blue Jay meeting. When Miss Seely blew her whistle and looked the twenty Jays over like a general inspecting the troops, her eagle eye saw right off that Sandy was missing.

"Where's Sandra?" she barked. She always barked. It was just her way, and the girls were used to it.

"We don't know," Addie answered, a little faster and louder than she meant to. She knew, and Irma and Ellen knew, but they were sworn to follow Sandy's orders.

"Well, we'll just have to go on without her, though why the leader of the Wolf Patrol isn't here unless she's really sick— and she's never sick—is beyond me." Miss

Seely looked put out. The Blue Jays hadn't been in existence until March, and she was new to the business of troop-captain. She got pretty nerved up when things didn't go the way she'd planned.

We went through our marching drills with Miss Seely barking out the orders. "Squads right. Squads left. About face. At ease." The bunch went through the motions, but our minds were on Sandy and what would happen if she got caught.

There was a pretty good chance that she would, because her house was right opposite the Y.W.C.A. on the gym side.

Sandy told our bunch where she was going when we stopped in at her house as usual on meeting day. Her mother always had some chocolate cake or molasses cookies or hermits on tap. Whichever it was, was good. Ordinarily we made short work of doing away with it and went on to the meeting fully revived — but not on this day.

Sandy had said her piece flatly. "I'm just not going to that silly old meeting. Marching up and down. Making knots. Counting up points for spying where barnacles grow. 'Blue Jay's honor' — my aching back! I'll bet not a one of us ever laid eyes on half the birds we say we've seen. I'm going fishing, and that's all about it."

We'd worked and worked on her to change her mind, but she wouldn't budge.

"So what are we going to tell Miss Seely when she asks where you are?" Addie was practical as usual. She was on Sandy's side and always would be, but she had to be prepared with a workable way to show it.

"Tell her I've come down with a bad case of the heebie-jeebies or leprosy or St. Vitus Dance." Sandy was being Sandy, talking up a storm and enjoying its effects. "Oh, all right," she said with one of her quick right-about-faces. "Tell her you don't know. After all, you don't know *where* I'm going. You just know *what for*."

We'd had to settle for that. We were scared, but we

felt pretty much as Sandy did. Saturdays in the old days before we got organized into Blue Jays used to be real adventures: going Mayflowering or lady's slippering in the spring; getting up a Larkin's soap order for a Flexible Flyer sled; digging dandelion greens to sell to our mothers' friends for twenty cents a basket when the going rate was fifteen cents; baking potatoes under upside-down plant pots, the smoke coming up through the pot-bottom chimney holes; or going fishing from one of the wharves for pollock or flounders. There was always something good to do and a lot more fun than going through this Blue Jay "rig-a-ma-role" even though the uniforms did make us feel pretty important.

The meeting was almost over. Miss Seely was giving out assignments for the week when Gladys squeaked. She never missed a chance to squeak and then squeal whenever she could stir up trouble. "Oh, Miss Seely! Look out the window! There's Sandy!" She pointed wildly.

Miss Seely looked and saw. She turned the color of beets. There was Sandy in middy blouse and bloomers, ambling home with a string of flounders hanging from a pole slung over her shoulder.

"Patrol come to order," she barked. "You will meet here on Thursday afternoon at four o'clock for the court-martial of Sandra Jellison for failing to live up to the Blue Jay code of honor. Dismissed."

We were a down-in-the-mouth bunch when we left the gym with Gladys squeaking in high-C range, "What do you want to bet that Sandy gets kicked out?" She was up in the clouds at the prospect. It wasn't that she had it in for Sandy, but at last something big was going to happen in Bar Harbor.

After plenty of pulling and hauling, the bunch agreed not to tell Sandy until after school on Monday. Sunday was bad enough, getting decked out in church clothes, sitting through Parson Kittredge's going on and on about sin and the devil, hanging around the rest of the day doing nothing worthwhile because our families were bound and determined to "observe the Sabbath as the day of rest."

But Monday afternoon came and now Sandy knew. It was up to Addie to make sure that she turned up for her court-martial on Thursday.

It took some doing on Addie's part.

"Who cares?" Sandy said straight from the shoulder. I went fishing because I wanted to. I won't go to the old court-martial if I don't want to. Let them kick me out. See if I care."

But Addie wasn't one to give up. "I asked Miss Seely how it works. She said she'd pick a jury to hear the evidence and let them make up their minds. Come on, Sandy. It'll be like the moving pictures. You'll be on trial, and we'll get you off. It'll be a great show. You don't want to miss out on it."

To everyone's surprise, Sandy gave in. She wasn't exactly sold on the idea, but if the Blue Jays were finally going to do something interesting, she guessed she'd show up.

Then it was Thursday, and the Blue Jays were all in the gym. Miss Seely had dug up an old table and some folding chairs and set them up under the climbing ropes.

"This is the court-martial of Sandra Jellison for failing to live up to the Blue Jay code of honor," she said, spacing out the words. Her face looked spotted and clay colored. "I appoint Ellen Robertson, Gladys Joy, and Pauline Bragdon to review the case. Please go forward and take the seats behind the table. Sandra Jellison, you will sit in the chair opposite them. Answer all questions directly and volunteer no other information."

Irma and Addie fidgeted. "Why'd she have to go and pick Ellen?" Irma whispered behind her hand. "She's too bashful to talk up. Now if *I* had it to do . . ."

The court-martial began.

Gladys (squeaking louder than ever): Where were you at meeting time last Saturday?

Sandy (lying back in her chair the way we all did at the picture show): Fishing down off Ladd's wharf.

Pauline: Did you go before meeting time?

Sandy: Sure. I went right after dinner.

Gladys: Did you figure to be back for meeting?

Sandy: No. Nate Osgood said the flounders were biting real lively. I wasn't coming home until I had a big enough haul for supper.

Gladys: Is that any way for a Blue Jay to act?

Sandy: Well, I don't know what's so awful about going fishing. Do you?

Around and around they went, getting nowhere. Ellen hadn't once opened her mouth. She looked done in, as if she'd been running too hard and couldn't get enough air.

Miss Seely brought them up short at 4:30. "This has gone on long enough. The reviewers will now vote on the evidence. If it shows Sandra to be guilty of conduct unsuitable for a Blue Jay, you will ask her to turn in her badge."

The old gym was quiet. This was a solemn moment. The Blue Jays knew it was all up for Sandy. She hadn't helped herself any by the way she'd answered. The seconds stretched out tight. You could almost smell the tension.

Suddenly Ellen sat up straight and looked them all in the eye. "I want to say something," she began. "I want to say that I don't think we ought to be making out that Sandy is a villain. We all of us know her. She's maybe the best of us all. When did she ever do a mean thing to anybody? When did you ever catch her telling a real lie? When she gives you her word, she never goes back on it. Maybe she shouldn't have gone fishing, but what she did wasn't half as bad as most of us do all the time. Sandy is good. If we make out that she isn't, we're the ones who are guilty. I vote that we go home. I've had enough of this dumb court-martial."

We sat there stunned. We'd never heard Ellen say more than a few words in a row, and what she'd said was the honest truth. We looked at Miss Seely. She was fumbling around with her whistle, yanking it up and down on its cord, and she didn't seem to want to say a thing. We looked at Sandy, and what we saw, we'd never forget. Sandy was crying!

Nobody said another word. We just got up and went out of the gym.

It wasn't until the bunch of us got together at Sandy's house after the court-martial that we found out why she had cried.

"Were you really sorry?" Addie asked.

"Sorry?" Sandy had an apple in her hand. She was studying it, turning it around and around as if she'd never seen one before.

We exchanged puzzled glances. Sandy wasn't acting like Sandy.

When she looked up, her eyes were brimming, but her mouth had the old deviltry-twist. "Sorry?" she repeated. "Who said anything about sorry? I just didn't know what you really thought about me until Ellen said what she said. I'm not sorry. I'm just glad!"

We Cross Our Bar—
Not Theirs

When the day was pretty and the tide was right, we were drawn to crossing the bar. For us, the expedition had all the magnetic pull of swimming the English Channel or scaling Mt. Everest. It was Adventure With Peril, and we loved the scared-excited feeling of even thinking about it.

The bar lay in the harbor between our village and Bar Island. When the tide was full, it vanished under water. When the tide was all the way out, it rose as if by magic out of the deep, a long strip of mussel-covered sharp-pebbled shoal. To cross the bar was to stumble and flinch, to yelp and yowl, to limp bruised and bloody across to another world, a world where lived only birds and beach grass, pines and spruce, granite ledge and sea wrack. I think we believed that we possessed the island, but the truth of the matter was that it possessed us, so strong, so irresistible was its attraction.

But it could be ours and we its for only as long as the tide was low. When the shore rock began darkening, it was time to start back. Otherwise, like the bar itself, we would vanish into the sea. The turn of the tide we saw as a jealous and interfering interloper who wouldn't let us be. But even so, part of our entranced delight in the whole journey was the lurking danger of being caught by the tide. We knew we wouldn't let it happen, but just suppose . . .

Back on home ground, our Adventure With Peril behind us, there was still time to see what was going on in the everyday world. To get up from the shore to the street, we had to pass by the wire fence that enclosed the public side of the Swimming Club pool. That fence was there to keep us apart from the summer colony, whose club it was. Still, it couldn't keep us from looking, and look we did, our eyes round with wonder.

Around that pool and in it disported the rusticator ladies, dressed to the nines for their afternoon appearances. I remember that I never wondered where the men were — perhaps off on the private golf course — so bemused I was by the ladies. As we saw it, they were there to swim, but we were baffled about how they could manage it: every one of them wore, in and out of water, a wide-brimmed hat, a dress with billowing skirts, long stockings, and, in some cases, gloves that reached from their fingers to their shoulders. Our eyes would travel a circuit of the pool, focus on the swimmers, and see that what we doubted we were seeing was true. They were doing a bogged-down breast stroke.

From where we stood, fingers locked in the wire mesh to keep our focus steady, what we saw was a rainbowed garden of flowered hats almost surrounded by rings of ballooning skirts. It was a pretty picture, funny but pretty, and we were glad we could see it before we went up the hill to the street and home.

We were well content with our day. We'd crossed our bar, and though we couldn't cross theirs, we wouldn't want to anyway. Their island was too fancy, too dressed-up, just plain too uncomfortable for us. We'd settle for what we had, torn feet and all. Outside the wire fence we were free.

The Ferry

In the days before a bridge tied our island to the mainland, the coming and going of the ferry boats provided daily free entertainment — not in a class with *The Perils of Pauline* and *The Clutching Hand*, which the ticket-taker at the Star Theater always let us slip in to see the ends of after school — but it served us well on Saturday mornings and late afternoons when nothing more overwhelming offered.

Still, I remember one Friday morning when the ferry provided more than the usual entertainment. School was closed that day for a teachers' convention. The whole faculty would be taking the *Norumbega*, the bigger and prettier sister ship of the *Schoodic*, from the village wharf to Mount Desert, where they'd get on the train for Portland. That would be a leave-taking we would not care to miss. Teachers out of school on a school day? Teachers all done up in traveling clothes, going away from us instead of coming toward us? Teachers set apart from our world by journeying to the big city over 150 miles away?

The boat would pull out at nine. We were there at eight-thirty, lined up on the wharf right where on other days we perched with feet hanging over the edge, fishing for flounders. We didn't say much. Anticipation kept us quiet.

"They coming yet?"

"No sign."

"They coming now?"

"Not yet."

"You don't suppose . . ."

But we didn't have to. The teachers were a dark mass moving onto the pier, coming toward us on their way to going away from us. And they were invested with strangeness: people in city clothes, chatting and smiling, looking years younger, free and softened. For the first time we were seeing them the way they looked when they weren't being teachers. It was a revelation not altogether comfortable because we couldn't wear into it so fast. I suppose that without thinking about it, we'd always seen them as ordained to live for us only. Now we had to move over. Their journey would put more than geographical miles between us.

They went up the gangplank.

The ropes were cast loose from bollards and bitts.

The whistle blew.

The boat was moving.

"Goodbye," we called.

They waved.

Then we couldn't see them any more. The boat was turning and heading out to sea as we watched.

Long Journey

G uess I'll go down to the store," she said to herself, and then because the words had come out loud enough for anyone to hear, she took a quick look around the coat corridor. The kids had all gone. "Good thing," she said in relief. This time the words stayed inside her head.

When she tried stomping into her overshoes the way her father and brothers did, her ankle twisted and turned over. "Gee, that makes me mad," she whispered, feeling for a moment less empty because she was mad. Her back pushed hard against the wall to keep her balance, she pulled and tugged at the black things until she got them on. "Not going to wear my beanie, though," she told her mother, who wasn't there.

Her coat buttoned only halfway down and her mittens dangling out of the pockets, she tiptoed over to her homeroom for a last peek to make sure. The shades were drawn down level. The teacher's desk was all picked up ready for the next morning. "Wonder where she went, anyway."

Suddenly a big hand clapped over her eyes. It smelled dusty and stale like her brothers' sweaters.

"Bet you don't know who this is," came a muffled voice from behind her.

"No, and I bet I wouldn't want to if I did," she flashed back without thinking.

"Awright for you, Miss Smarty, if you're going to be like that."

The hand gave up. She wheeled around. It was Tubby Connors. "Smarty yourself and see how you like it," she said balefully, stamping a foot.

"Well, gee." He was trying to glare back at her, but his bottom lip was sticking out, and his face was as red as if she'd slapped him. "I just wanted to know if you're going to walk home."

"I most certainly am going to walk home when I get around to it." She yanked her mittens out of her pockets, waved them to show she meant business, gave the middle button of her coat a decisive slap, and pushed past him out the side door.

"Boys," she spluttered, "always hanging around."

A lump of snow lay in her path. She gave it a good kick, felt better for a minute, and then, remembering that she wouldn't see Miss Godwin again until next morning, she stood still, not wanting to go to the store, not wanting to go home, not wanting to go anywhere.

The winter light was already turning the mountains blue. Other times, she would have liked the blueness and the cold, the frozen footprints under her feet, and her breath smoking out before her if she'd been walking with the teacher.

Instead, she stood still, afraid of the afternoon because she was alone in it. It was too big. It rushed across to get inside her, and there was such a tightness all over her that she couldn't take it in.

Her hands made fists in her mittens. She thrust them deep down in her pockets, shook her head as if to shake free of the tightness, and moved on, away from the school.

Outside Carpenter's store she fingered the nickel in her pocket. Maybe if she got a nickel's worth of Mary Janes, she'd feel better.

"What's the matter, Jennie?" Mr. Carpenter asked her, peering over the tops of his glasses. "Lost your best friend?"

She hated to be called Jennie, but today it didn't seem to matter. "No, I guess not," she said listlessly. "I'd like five Mary Janes, Mr. Carpenter."

While he was reaching into the case, she looked around from force of habit to see if she could tell where the dark, wet smell was coming from, the smell she'd never been able to give a name to. It wasn't just the black mounds of liver on the meat block or the pickles floating in their slimy brine. And it wasn't the candy, no matter how old her mother said it was, because then it would taste smelly, and it didn't. Oh well, she really didn't care where it came from today.

Out in the snowy twilight again, she pulled the yellow and red wrapper off a Mary Jane, stuck the whole molasses slab in her mouth, bit through it fast to get the golden taste of the peanut butter, and was doggedly comforted. You didn't feel quite so lonesome when you had something good to eat.

Oh good, she thought as she crossed the street, they haven't turned the lights on yet. There was something she liked about being in her father's store at this time of winter day: leaning up against the front door, her breath clouding the glass, the dim, quiet cave of the store stretching out behind her, nobody saying much because there never seemed much to say when the day was changing into night, watching the lights come on across the street — sometimes one at a time, sometimes in clusters — feeling queer because another day was slipping into the dark and wondering where it went, feeling solemn and more grown-up than she would have dared show anyone except Miss Godwin, feeling trembly and religious and happy and sad all at once, feeling good and feeling glad because she felt so full of goodness.

As she scuffed the snow off her overshoes and pulled open the door, she had another of those queer moments of understanding when it seemed as if someone outside herself were explaining herself to her. "That's why you wanted to come to the store this afternoon," the someone said. "You knew you could get Big Feelings, but unless you can keep having them by yourself, not just when you're thinking of Miss Godwin, you won't ever know whether what you're feeling is the things themselves or her."

That thought took her by surprise.

"Hello, Pug," she said to her big brother, who was sitting on the counter by the cash register, hugging his knees and looking into space.

"What do you want?" he asked suspiciously. "Because if you're after a nickel, you won't get it. I haven't sold a thing all day."

"I don't want anything," she said with unusual meekness. "I don't want anything at all."

"Well, that's lucky because you wouldn't get it, anyway," he said with a big-brother grin in his voice. He was trying to get a rise out of her, but she didn't feel like bothering.

Her ears were beginning to throb the way they always did when she came in out of the cold, and there were prickly little chills running up and down her legs. She leaned against the door, drew a picture in the fog her breath made on the glass, looked out across the snowy street, and watched the last thin light grow dimmer and dimmer.

The feeling was beginning to come. It was a mournful feeling, all right, but you knew you didn't have to feel it if you didn't want to. It was the difference between the far-off sadness you felt when you heard that your grandfather, who had meant no more than a wet kiss and a pat on the head, had died, and what you'd feel if anything happened to your little black cocker. Even though it was proper to feel sad about your grandfather, you could stop any time you wanted to. But if Snipper died, you'd never, never, never be able to run away from the hurting.

"What are you so droopy about?" Pug's voice, cutting suddenly across her thinking, startled her.

"Pug," she said on a quick impulse, her heart jumping like crazy because she'd never said anything like this to him before, "tell me some of the big things you think!"

"Don't be such a little mutt," he growled, not unkindly.

She turned back to the window and just stood there. It's no use, she thought, they'll never talk about the things that go on inside their heads.

"Come on, snap out of it," Pug said after a while. "Go buy yourself some jellybeans." He was tapping a coin on the counter. "Take it and beat it. I got things to do."

The nickel wasn't what she wanted. Still, Pug was trying to be nice. She took it, said, "Thanks, Pug. Bye," and went out into the cold darkness.

Suddenly, as she plodded along, her face held down against the wind from the mountains, she struck ice, slipped, and righted herself just in time to keep from falling. "Good thing it's dark," she said aloud, not even bothering to look around to see if anyone could hear. Sheltered by the darkness, she inched along — "like an old lady," she told herself. It would be a relief to be grown up; then you could show you were afraid of ice and no one would make fun of you.

Halfway up Main Street she paused by Miss Whitmore's window. It was frosted like the others, but she knew what was inside: three gleaming cases of caramels, gumdrops, chocolates, taffy, and jellybeans. With a nickel, if you knew what to ask for, you could buy enough to fill a bag more than half full. She pushed open the door, heard the little bell jangling in the back room, and then, just as she always did, Miss Whitmore pit-patted out, the same twitchy smile on her face, the same rabbity look in her eyes. Usually it took a long time to decide, but tonight it was easy. Jellybeans had sounded good when Pug mentioned them; that's what she wanted.

She watched intently while Miss Whitmore filled the penny cup five times. All the kids said Old Lady Whitmore would slice a gumdrop in half for exact measure. But she wasn't skimping tonight. The jellybeans made a satisfying clashing noise as they fell against each other in the pink-and-purple-striped bag. And she even threw in a licorice one before she twisted the bag shut and passed it over the counter. It was certainly a lucky night for going to Miss Whitmore's.

Outside the shop she loafed along while she counted the jellybeans: "Sixty-four, sixty-five, sixty-six!" That was more than she'd ever get anywhere except at Fred Lederer's when he'd been drinking.

It was hard to eat in solid comfort and creep along the ice at the same time, yet she was surprised when she noticed that she'd already reached the village green. The town clock said quarter past four. Was that all it was? It had been such a long afternoon.

The village green had frozen up for the winter: the fountains covered, the bandstand boarded in, the crab apple tree looking stiff and lonely like a crippled old orphan. Still, she felt twice as safe there now than she did in summer.

In winter, when the cold drove everyone indoors, she could stay home and read and think without being noticed; nobody called her a queer kid or told her to run outside and get some air into her lungs. But all through the summer months, everyone made for the village green on band concert nights. Whenever she could, she stayed away, not liking the squeaky giggling the girls did to show off before the boys; not liking the whispery restlessness there was in the air those nights. But sometimes shutting herself away in the house wasn't as happy a thing to do as she'd have liked it to be, because no matter how much you shrank away from the giggling and hollering, you hated to feel out of it. And how could you be sure you weren't a queer kid?

Passing by the library, she hesitated again. If she went to the poetry alcove and took down books with poems like the ones Miss Godwin had been reading aloud in class, she wouldn't do her lessons when she got home. She'd be too excited inside. And then she'd try writing some of the things she couldn't say to anybody — not even Miss Godwin – because when she wrote them or said them, they came out ragged and stumbling, and it wasn't fair to the niceness of what came into her head to say it so badly.

Then, walking as if in her sleep, she found herself going up the library steps, across the glass-floored hall, and into the big room.

The librarian nodded to her and smiled. That was because she wasn't being kicked out any longer for rattling candy bags. She couldn't imagine ever having wanted to do anything in the big room but read as fiercely as she did now. There were shelves and shelves of books she was dying to get her nose into.

She made her choice as fast as she could: *New Poems*, by Tennyson, because Miss Godwin had read them "The Lady of Shalott," and *A Dome of Many-Colored Glass* because the words in the name set her dreaming.

The minute she got outside, she did a kind of limping run over the icy sidewalk past the Y.W.C.A. and down the hill to her house.

When she tried the front door and found it locked, she pulled off a mitten and reached under the mat for the key. All the delivery boys and everyone else knew that was where it was kept, but her Mother always said she felt safer with the door locked when she was out.

The house was dark, warm, full of quietness.

She pulled the light cord in the kitchen. The brass faucets, polished so hard you could see your eye in them, shone jolly and beaming. The whole room was clean, trim, and fresh-smelling. When she came back to it at this time of day and found no one home, she always smiled at the kitchen, wanting to ask it if it had had a nice afternoon nap — it looked so rested and comfortable.

"Lessons first?" she asked herself, thinking of her poetry books. Then for no reason she could understand, Miss Godwin came back into her mind. Miss Godwin, poetry, thinking big thoughts — they were all one, and she could go on having them, and she could fall asleep tonight knowing that they would be there tomorrow.

"Bet there's fresh bread," she said suddenly, opening the bread drawer and wrinkling her nose in delight at the brown crispy smell. She pulled out a loaf, cut off the heel and the next piece, buttered them thickly, took one of the new books from the library, and went to sit in the dark by the window in the dining room rocker.

It was enough to hold the book against her, bite blissfully into the new bread, and look out the window at the mountains, which, although they showed black and rounded in the winter night, she didn't see at all because it was so lovely just to think.

Breaking Bread
with a Rusticator

If you were born and brought up in a famous Maine island resort in the early 1900s, you called the summer people "rusticators," and they called you "natives." Both terms could be used indulgently if the relationship was civil and — more important — profitable. Or they could be used as insult if either group failed to keep its proper social distance. The line of demarcation, though never to my knowledge drawn out loud, was an accepted fact of life.

But one year the local Y.W.C.A. conceived a plan of action by which the twain could meet in social amity — and the little children were to take the first steps. This miracle called for a mini-merger of the summer and local branches of the Girl Scouts, arranged by mail that spring.

Since I was one of the natives, I had no way of knowing how the summer girls felt about this experiment. As for our group, we were suspicious, gingerly willing, and uneasy. We never confessed our doubts to our friends, or even to ourselves; after all, Maine people pride themselves on being "as good as the next one." Nevertheless, I, for one, was not at all sure that we could even talk to the other group without disaster. To the rusticators, our downeast accents were "quaint"; to us their accents were "stuck up" and put on.

Whether my uneasiness ever got beyond concern about accents, I do not remember, but, in general, we village girls were uncomfortably aware of the immense difference between our family's bank accounts, houses, cars, boats, and styles of recreation — and theirs. For example, their "cottages" — which monopolized the entire shoreline — were Italian villas, French chateaus, stately English homes or, if less cosmopolitan, they were mammoth, rambling, "properly weathered" wooden edifices with acres of lawns, tennis courts, stables, docks, gardens, and scrupulously manicured driveways. All that could be said of our houses was that they stood up against the savagery of Maine winters and sheltered the storekeepers, gardeners, carpenters, plumbers, masons, and laundresses who served the summer folk.

The initial step in the cross-pollination experiment was to take the form of a nature hike and picnic in the woods. We were to bring our own lunches. That part of the plan, at least, was reassuring. We knew how to handle our own food; theirs, which could conceivably include such exotics as the artichokes and alligator pears their parents ordered through our markets, would have posed a coping problem we were in no way equipped to resolve.

When we assembled in the Y.W.C.A. gym on the day of the hike, we natives were clumped together for mutual protection, a garrison troop frozen into combat readiness. The summer girls, who had arrived in their chauffeur-driven cars, might have come from another planet where war, or rumor of war, had never threatened. They were laughing, calling out to each other, riding high on high spirits. They talked — yes, they talked — but only to each other. We stood stiffly silent, watching them. At this point the experiment in détente seemed headed for disaster.

However, the nature walk was so regimented that it allowed for no advance, retreat, attack, or cessation of hostilities. The lady in charge, a summer girl's governess, had laid down the law before we left the gym. We were not to talk while we walked. We were to listen to her tell us about the trees and the mosses, the birds and the insects — and we were to "Observe!"

We observed willingly enough, but we mostly observed each other — though there was not much to be gained from what we saw. In our Scout uniforms we all looked pretty much alike except that the natives sported curls, whereas the rusticators wore their hair in braids. At least we had more leeway in that important respect.

My concern about the difference in accents was proving to be no stumbling block to communication. Not only were we not allowed to talk, we had simply no interest in preprandial conversation. We wanted lunch; we needed lunch; our minds were on our stomachs.

When at last we were permitted to break ranks for the picnic we plunked down fast. I landed on a good-sized boulder and was just settling myself with a big sigh of relief when Augusta Nichols dropped down beside me. I knew who she was from seeing her around in the village and from having her pointed out as the daughter of multimillionaire Archibald Nichols. The Nicholses' summer home, "Belleview," which commanded a view of the whole bay, had inspired one of our local wits to call his own place, which commanded a view of nothing, "No View."

We darted sidelong looks at each other. She said, "Hello." I said, "Hi." And that exchange terminated our social intercourse.

Too hungry to care, I opened my shoebox and rummaged through its contents with satisfaction: pot roast sandwiches, stuffed eggs, a big wedge of chocolate cake with fudge frosting, some molasses cookies, doughnuts, a couple of bananas. My mother and all my friends' mothers always saw to it that we had enough picnic fodder to support life comfortably.

I was munching away happily on my first sandwich and had gotten far enough into it to be curious about Augusta's lunch when I noticed that was she fumbling around untying a small bag that hung on a string from her uniform's belt.

"Aren't you starved?" I blurted out. "Where's your lunch?" Clearly the subject of food was taking precedence over my qualms about communication.

She looked at me and then at the bag. "This is it," she said miserably. She opened the bag and took out two hard-boiled eggs.

"Is that all you *want*?" I simply couldn't believe what I was seeing. This starvation-diet could be another, more insuperable, barrier to overcoming our differences.

The expression on her face was a queer mixture of anger and embarassment. "Of course it isn't all I want. It's all I could get! Cook didn't want to be bothered. This is all she'd give me."

Well! If anyone had told me that this was the way a daughter of the rich had to live, I'd have said he was heading for the state asylum. But this was the way it was, and here was I, whose father had a hard time making the summer money last through the winter, feeling sorry for her, whose father was a millionaire!

"Have some," I said, passing over the shoebox. "There's too much for me."

The last sentence was a long way from the truth. I just thought it would sound too much like bragging if I said, "There's plenty."

"Oh, thanks ever so much! It looks awfully good." She was smiling now, and if I hadn't known the difference, I'd have said she was just one of us hungry kids who'd suffered a nature walk for the picnic at the end.

And then we were talking as easily and naturally as if there were no differences between us.

When I asked her how she'd liked the nature hike, she looked sideways, her mouth pulled down, her eyes grinning.

"You too?" I asked, delighted. "Did you ever in your life have to listen to so much nothing as that lady was giving out? 'OBSERVE!' " I picked up a pine needle, held it up as high as I could reach, pulled in my breath, and let out a long "AH-h-h-h. This is a specimen of the pine needle family — very rare, very be-you-ti-ful!"

We doubled up in wild and zany laughter.

And so for the two of us, the merger of rusticator with native was a that-day success. Thanks to the great leveler, food, we had crossed the line of demarcation.

Other Times,
Other Wheels

There was a time when "wheels" meant something quite different from modern-day automobiles and motorcycles. In the years before World War I, the carts and wagons that traveled our island's roads were — at least for the children of our village — a continuing source of drama and delight.

If we move from now to then, the then becomes the now as I tell it . . .

"Tally-ho!" comes to us on the wind of horses passing and a spectacular vision gallops by. Four or six or eight paired horses, harnesses gleaming, are couriers of a long high chariot driven by picture men in hunting pinks with white stocks and black velvet caps. Men standing, burnished horns to lips, sound the imperious "Tally-Ho!" — the wondrous annunciation.

Down Main Street, from the edge of the sea toward the distant mountains, they move, proud, aloof, clothed in their lordly splendor.

It is summer, of course, and the unquenchable summer people are playing prodigal games — playing with imagination and laughter, in the mad, glad world they create.

Behind them plods the lowly sprinkler, its arms wetting down the dust in sideways arcs of spray. Decorous, useful, sensible, putting things to rights after the children finish playing.

It is still morning. If we hurry, we may catch up with the ice-wagon on one of the side streets. There is no way to know if he's still making his rounds except to scurry up one street and down another looking for where a trail of waterdrops has pitted the ground in a straight line toward somebody's back door. If the pitting is dark enough, the wagon has just been there. Rush, pant, tangle our feet, get there in time — and there it is, a huge rectangle on wheels, its back open, its insides spilling out sawdust. The iceman strides back from the house, tongs dangling loosely from his load-free hand.

If we stand still, look up at him, and wait mutely, he jerks his head up and down once, spreads open the tongs, sets them wide around whichever one of the great ice blocks come closest to hand and yanks it to the lip of the wagon.

We watch, transfixed. We've seen him do this before, but it is always the first time — the unfolding, the revelation.

He drops the tongs to one side and reaches for his hatchet of a pick. "Clink, clink, CHINK!" A rainbow-colored spray of ice-chips falls around and into our outstretched hands.

He slams the back door of his wagon shut, shoves a thick wooden pin through the hasp, clucks to his horse, and moves on, leaving us stuffing our mouths with frozen slivers. We suck in total bliss. Ours is the ice and the goodness thereof.

On the same day, or maybe on another, the junk man's rickety wagon looms into view, the worn-down horse crouching under the slapping reins. "Rags and bones. Any rags and bones?" His call is less a question than a signal that business can be done, all parties willing.

The cart creaks toward us, its wheels squeaking and squealing, its freight of rags and bones, rusty wire and cracked bottles grinding and clashing, rolling crazily in dizzy patterns from side to side, from end to end of the wagon.

We watch. We listen. We call to him. "How are you today, Mr. Higginbotham?"

He lifts the sweat-stained rim of his battered old hat, nods benevolently in our direction, and rattles on.

We wave. He is gone. It was a pleasant encounter.

Cut-unders pass us by, each with two softly padded seats for four passengers under a canopy of waving fringe. They offer no surprises. Their drivers are business bound, eyes fixed on the road to their destination. They are the horse-drawn taxis. We walk.

We walk in search of the organ grinder and his monkey. The monkey is our friend even though he gets money for what we aren't allowed to do — climb all over people, tweak their noses, tug at their hair, stick out his hand for pennies and, clutching them in his little fist, scuttle off, grinning. He is our friend in a world of grownups who can't understand why we want to act like monkeys.

The organ on wheels has what we know but can never believe: a voiced locked inside, a voice that breaks free, singing, when the crank goes round. Like a dazzle in the mind, the song begins a light-filled dream that shimmers on the horizon, bursts in a moment of impossible magnificence, and then is gone. In reality the organ is scabby, shabby, scrofulous — but not in our eyes. To us it is a box on wheels that sings the romance of a faraway country in a language much softer than our own, full of longing, full of dreaming! A miracle it is when the dark little organ grinder in the dusty purple suit puts his brown fingers around the crank, starts winding in a slow circle, and out comes the full-voiced singing. *"O sole mio, O sole mio."* We feel what it says without understanding the words. And when the singing stops, we are glad that the pennies come showering down. The monkey claws for them in the dust. The organ grinder laughs and bows, throws a general kiss, and then is gone.

The Tally-ho, the sprinkler, the ice-wagon, the junk cart, the cut-unders, the barrel-organ — they were all there in that lost time, all of them on wheels, all of them moving in and out of our days, part of the stir and wonder of our living.

But the set of wheels we gave our hands and mouths and hearts to was the tarring-wagon — yes, the tarring wagon that laid wide sheets of shining, nose-tingling, thick black stickiness across the roads. It came after the Tally-ho days. It was Progress, or so we gathered from our parents who'd waited long for the moment to come when they could glide along, dressed in their holiday best, free from clouds of gritty dust. (After all, the sprinkler had only one horse and two arms. It couldn't be expected to be dampening the road everywhere at all times!)

That tar! Odes have been written to nightingales, west winds, Grecian urns, Billie Joe — fine things all — but they are not in a class with black tar: tar you can smell and taste and chew, or set your feet down into, leaving immortal prints. Spruce gum, the gift of spring in the woods, was one thing — good enough and more until we chewed tar. That was the Fourth of July in comparison with Valentine's day. That was hot, thick, sticky, smelly heaven.

The tarring-wagon rumbled like the rumble of an about-to-break thunderstorm. From far off we heard it coming. We felt the earth shake under our feet as it crept toward us, huge, black, steaming. Do I remember that it whistled out of a chimney high aloft its monster body? Who knows? All we knew was that *it* had come, bearing free riches of lovely tar.

Wheels. In my latter years I need them, use them, depend on them — but never without a sense of desolate loss for time when wheels were part of the color, drama, romance of my living.

Twelfth Summer

It was going to be another of those Sunday picnics out at Marshall Pond. She hated them.

Her mother always got so stirred up about the baked beans and cabbage salad, the deviled eggs and pot-roast sandwiches, her special piccalilli and her secret recipe for marble cake that the house was in an uproar from getting-up time until they started out.

Then came the stowing away of all the food and sweaters and Sunday paper in the trunk of the Staffords' old Franklin.

And that was another thing. They always went with the Staffords because her family didn't have a car. And Mr. Stafford always drove as if he was going to a funeral. And he always smoked long black cigars. And she always got sick from the smell and being wedged in so tight between Mrs. Stafford and her mother in the back seat.

When they finally got to Marshall Pond and unloaded the car and, after a lot of pulling and hauling, settled on the warmest-coolest sunniest-shadiest spot to have the picnic, there was nothing for her to do.

All her gang were out at Loon Lake, swimming and

eating hot dogs and roaring around like wild Indians, as her mother called them. When she tried to explain why it wasn't fair that they could go, and she couldn't, her mother got huffy. "Now don't argue, Sarah. You're twelve years old and ought to know better. If the Staffords are good enough to take us as a family, the least you can do is be part of it for one day a week."

There was no use saying that her brothers didn't have to go. They were out at the golf club, caddying and getting rich on summer people's tips. She knew what her mother would say. "That's different. They're *boys*," as if that gave them a free ride to heaven while she was stuck with a lot of old people out at Marshall Pond, where you couldn't swim because they said it wasn't safe, and there was nothing for her to do.

But this Sunday turned out to be different.

Just around the bend from where the picnic party had settled she came upon a flat-bottomed rowboat. Well, now! If there were oars . . . There were. She yanked off her sneakers and socks, untied the mooring line, shoved off, and jumped in.

For a few careful minutes she rowed hard, hugging the shore away from where the picnic was being set out. When she judged that she was out of eye-reach, she took a deep breath and headed for the middle of the pond where the sun was making a shining dazzle.

"This is something like it," she told herself when she got there. She pulled in the oars and stretched out flat, drinking in the wonder of escape, of being where they couldn't get at her, of being in a world of her own, easy and free. She closed her eyes and saw a blaze of red and black from looking too long at the sun. The boat rocked gently. She was falling asleep.

Suddenly she heard a voice calling, hoarse and thick. "Help . . . oh, help!" She sat up and looked. Not far away, she saw a head bobbing. Then a hand stretched up from the water. Then nothing.

She grabbed the oars and rowed as hard as she could.

The head came up again, hair plastered flat and streaming water.

She was almost there . . . There! "Come on, take my hand. Hold on."

It was a man. He looked at her, his eyes rolling, not seeing her hand.

"You're all right. Here." She pushed the blade of an oar to where he was. "Hang on. Take it easy."

His eyes stopped rolling. "Tired, so tired," he mumbled, but he reached for the oar and was treading water feebly.

She wasn't strong enough to pull him into the boat. "Look, I'll row you in. You just hang on."

He caught hold of the back of the boat.

She rowed him in.

A small crowd had collected on the shore: her parents, the Staffords, and a bunch of other picnickers she hadn't seen around. They were clumped together waiting, not talking, just waiting.

After they'd helped the man to dry ground, things started moving like a movie running out of control. They all talked at once, no one listening to anyone else.

Now that it was over, she figured she was in for big trouble — sneaking away, taking the boat, going out on the pond.

But it wasn't that way at all. They were making a fuss over her and making out that she was a heroine like in *The Perils of Pauline*. It was crazy. She hadn't done much. Anyone who wasn't half-witted would have done the same. But it was a long sight better being a heroine than twelve-year-old Sarah Guptill, who'd thought she'd catch it.

The man turned out to be Albert Hamor, who clerked in Goodwin's shoe store. She'd seen him around but hadn't paid much attention. He was one of the older crowd, all in their twenties. His path and hers had no reason to cross.

But now he was looking at her as if she was something

special. And he was saying over and over, "You saved my life, Sarah Guptill. You — saved — my — life." And before she knew what was going to happen, he'd grabbed hold of her and was hugging her as if he'd never let go.

That was when it happened, an explosion in her middle like nothing she'd ever known. Albert Hamor and Sarah Guptill. It wasn't the Sheik of Araby looking as if he'd die without her in his arms, but it felt like that, and she knew she'd never be the same.

In the weeks that followed, she went through the usual motions but she wasn't really awake. She was sleepwalking, dreaming.

She took to walking slowly down Main Street, pausing at Goodwin's shoe store to study the window display, which wasn't interesting. Her eyes kept looking up over the shoes to the inside of the store. When she was lucky, she caught a glimpse of Albert Hamor, mostly the top of this head as he sat on the stool fitting shoes.

Once he saw her, waved, and mouthed something she, of course, couldn't hear, but from the size of his smile, she knew he was remembering Marshall Pond, and she felt him hugging her again.

The sleepwalking and dreaming went on. Her mother seemed to be always shaking her head in despair. "I don't know what's got into Sarah," she heard her telling her father. "She acts like she's coming down sick."

"Well, she's twelve," her father said, sounding as sensible as he always did. "Isn't it about time?"

About time for what? She didn't know what he meant, and it didn't much matter.

What did matter was that it was about time for the Old Timers Ball, which happened every August. The year before, you couldn't have dragged her to it, but now was different. Way down under her thoughts, something she didn't recognize was stirring. Sarah Guptill at the ball. Albert Hamor steering a straight path in her direction. Albert Hamor bowing, putting out his hand to her and saying, "May I have the pleasure of this dance?" And away they would go out onto the floor, he in his dark blue suit and dazzling white shirt, she in her pale pink organdy with the swirly skirt — the dress her mother had bought for her birthday that she'd looked at with such horror. "*Me* wearing *that?*" she'd yelled inside herself. But she'd made herself say, "Thank you," hoping it sounded as if she meant it, and promptly hid it away in the darkest corner of her closet.

But that was then. This was now. She saw herself gliding and twirling in a pale pink mist, Albert Hamor's eyes fastened on hers as if they'd never let go.

The night of the ball came. Once her parents had recovered from the shock of hearing her say she wanted to go, things began moving fast. She'd start out with them, of course, but from little things they said, she knew they'd let loose of her once they got there. They were treating her with kid gloves these days.

The Casino, where all the basketball games and dances took place, looked like a fairyland to her, with crepe-paper streamers draped in scallops from the ceiling lights, rubber plants filling in the corners, the stage set up like a round bandstand with Japanese lanterns sending soft-colored lights all over the hall.

She danced with Joe and Dave and Billy, who were in her grade at school. They went through their regular antics, making funny faces and then laughing uproariously, bumping into other couples and acting put upon when they got told off. She sleepwalked through the dances, her eyes circling the hall, looking, looking . . .

When she'd almost given up, she saw him coming in through the street door. Dark blue suit, dazzling white shirt, his hair, which she'd once seen streaming water, combed in a waving pompadour. He was laughing and talking with Gracie Adams, who worked in the bank across from Goodwin's store. They were holding hands.

"I'm thirsty," she said to her partner. "Let's get some punch."

He steered her over to the refreshment table, ladled

out a cupful of raspberry shrub, and shoved it in the direction of her hand.

Sarah was drinking shakily, nose down in the cup, when she felt a hand coming down over her shoulder from behind.

"Sarah Guptill, I do believe." It was Albert, and he was circling around to stand before her, Albert smiling and holding out his hand. "Gracie, this is the young lady who saved my life. If it hadn't been for her . . ."

Gracie took her other hand in both of hers. "Sarah," she said, "what you did — well, I don't know how to put it, but we all think you're the bravest and smartest little girl in town. If we can ever do something for you . . ."

"You can!" Sarah was shouting inside herself. "I'm *not* a little girl. Don't treat me like one!"

The music was starting up.

"Just remember," Albert said, "I owe my life to you." He was looking straight into her eyes. "And I'll never forget it."

And then he turned to Gracie. "May I have the pleasure of this dance?"

And away they went, gliding and twirling.

Heritage from War

World War I was over. People had been killed or maimed in the fighting. People had died from the Spanish Influenza. The world had changed.

But that year, most of us who were sophomores in a high school on a Maine island were little the wiser fools for the change.

Our homeroom teacher took pains to spell out the definition of sophomore for us at the beginning of the school year. We were not impressed. "Wise" sounded old and set in one's ways. "Fools" was a shoe that fitted us better, but we refused to put it on.

We lived from day to day, carelessly, taking no sober thought for the morrow — that is, until in our drifting we landed up hard against the rock — two people who had come back from the war to teach in our school.

On that opening day in September, Miss Davis looked wound-up tight and tired. She was wearing her gray blue yeoman's uniform. We figured that she must have just come off a transport ship from France.

Mr. Rivers, we heard, had been shell-shocked. He was a queer ashy yellow color, and he moved like a crab.

We were all eyes. These weren't teachers as we knew them; they simply didn't fit the mold. Thrown off base, we were polite and unusually obedient.

But it wasn't long before we realized that Miss Davis's class in English and Mr. Rivers's in French would either make us or break us. Neither knew the meaning of halfway measures.

Sloppy homework, lessons only partly prepared or not prepared at all drew long withering stares from Miss Davis. No scolding. No threatening. No detention after school. Just icy contempt.

Mr. Rivers blew up, turned white — then dark — and shook.

These deep freezes and emotional earthquakes were not easy to take. I, for one, began to wonder what would happen if we did some real work for a change. But wondering was as far as I was ready to go.

Then one day Mr. Rivers kept me after school to learn "The Marseillaise" the way he wanted it learned. I had memorized it without trouble but without worrying too much about meaning or accent.

"Would you for once try to do justice to a man's work?" he said, more quietly than usual. "It isn't enough to rattle it off like multiplication tables. A man cared with his whole soul for his native land. He was calling his people to arms in her service. He wrote from a glorious belief in her future. Think what you're saying, and say it with as much care as it deserves."

I tried.

He smiled. And suddenly he looked as if he had himself all together. "Yes. That's more nearly like it," he said. "And from now on you'll remember that language and the way it's used when it's used sincerely require the respectful attention of its readers."

That was a new idea to me. It not only made sense, it was exciting. I thought, too, that if a man who had been shell-shocked in the war could care enough about teaching us the right way to learn, the best we could do would be little enough.

Another day, when I happened to go early to English class, I found Miss Davis in tears. I was shocked and scared. She had always been so strong and dignified and in command of herself. "Excuse me," I said without really knowing what I was saying. "I'll come back later."

She reached out for my arm. "No, stay. I want you to read a poem by John McCrae," and she pointed to the book which lay open on her desk.

I looked down. The words took shape on the page:

> In Flanders fields the poppies blow
> Between the crosses row on row . . .

I looked up at Miss Davis. She was shaking her head as if to shake off the tears. "This book was just published. I thought I had put the war behind me, but the crosses — the crosses. Who can forget!"

Ignorant as I was of the war, I had heard of Flanders. And suddenly I saw the graves, the dead men lying beneath the crosses, the poppies blowing as if nothing had ever happened. I read on:

> We are the Dead. Short days ago
> We lived, felt dawn, and sunset glow,
> Loved, were loved, and now we lie
> In Flanders fields.

In that moment my world changed, and I began to see with more than my eyes. But I stood there like a lump. I could think of nothing fit to say, so I just stood there, looking dumbly at Miss Davis.

Then she smiled, and it was as if the sun had come out from behind an eclipse. "But we are the living," she said, "and we have a job to do together. Shall we set about doing it?"

I went to my seat and waited for class to begin. And while I knew that I was not yet wise, I knew that I was no longer a fool. My heritage from the war was two magnificent people who refused to settle for less than the best. My education had begun.

Juliet and Prohibition

Yesterday a young friend with a large bump of curiosity about the "olden days" asked me what it was like to live through Prohibition in our island village in Maine.

"Well, I guess you'd have to say it depended on what side you were on," I told him. "It was war, you know — no, you don't know — but I was in it, not fighting but getting burned by the fallout. No fun, my boy, no fun at all!"

And then and there I was back in 1920 with Juliet, the Grahams, and a basketball game that rocked the town like an explosion.

Prohibition was the powder keg. Juliet lit the fuse. It was her job, then, so I suppose we had no right to feel the way we did except that we thought we knew all there was to know about Juliet, and the evidence was strong against her.

Since Juliet played the leading role in that drama, what we'd call an antihero one today, she needs some thinking about. To do that I'll have to go back to when I first felt her outsized presence on our village streets.

From the days when I was not quite high enough to see over the counter of the General Delivery window at the post office, I was afraid of Juliet. She was a mountain of a woman with a deep, gruff voice. Her hair was clipped close to her head like a man's. She wore a man's cap, a tweed suit tailored exactly like a man's except for the skirt, men's shirts, four-in-hand ties. And she sported a cane. In her own way she was quite a dandy.

A silver badge on her lapel read S.P.C.A. When I asked my father what it meant, he told me that Juliet was a friend to all dumb animals and that she punished people who were mean to them.

You couldn't go down street without running across Juliet somewhere — in the barbershop, standing talking in a doorway, plunging along the sidewalk, buying a ticket at the Star Theater.

She went to the movies whenever the picture changed. And there, too, she made her presence felt in a pretty uncomfortable way. If you were unlucky enough to be ahead of her on the way in or out, you got the tip of her cane in the middle of your back, and the sharp force of the goad sent you and the ones ahead of you almost sprawling in the aisles. Along with the poking came a volley of abuse in a cloud-wave of alcoholic breath.

We thought it was pretty funny, under the circumstances, when Prohibition hit the country, and she was appointed Revenue Officer in our town, with the power to raid your house and arrest you if you had any liquor around.

But it wasn't funny when she invaded the Grahams' home one night, found a carafe of Scotch on the dining-room sideboard, and arrested our friends' father, a native-born Scot who never let a fellow-townsman across his threshold without according him the welcome of a wee dram.

What made the arrest more unfunny was the timing. It happened the night before our crucial basketball game, the one with Coney High, a big-city school that was way out of our class.

The Graham girls were our stars, the ones we'd hitched our wagon to. Jean was the center. Alix was the forward we fed the ball to for most of our score. Without them we hadn't a hope of winning.

Word of the arrest swept through the school like a brush fire in a high wind. The corridors were aflame with anger. That two-faced Judas of a Juliet! What right had she to stand in judgment? What right had she to ruin our team's chances of winning? For naturally we assumed that Jean and Alix would be kept home, or if they weren't, would be in no shape to keep their minds on the game. The whole town would turn out. Tongues would be wagging. The folks who lived in glass houses would relish throwing the first stones, even though there weren't many who hadn't reaped the illicit rewards of living on a coastal haven for rum-runners. And the decent people, the ones who made a habit of minding their own business, would sit there and just feel bad. Altogether, there was not much cause for rejoicing.

But the game was scheduled, and it would be played.

It was something to see the faces when the team ran out on the floor, and there were Jean and Alix, their heads high, their color a little flushed, their mouths tight with intention. They were there to play — for the team, for their father, for themselves.

I know it sounds like a tailored dime novel written in the days when a dime bought a hero's success story, but it really happened. Jean and Alix played an inspired game. The rest of us caught the sparks of their fire. We played Coney so hard they didn't know what hit them. And we won — 36 to 20.

Although the victory put the arrest into shadow, we kept on having murderous thoughts about Juliet for what she, of all whited sepulchers, did to Mr. Graham and almost did to our team. For a long time we, like Queen Victoria, were "not amused" by her and her cane, and the breath lozenges she chewed.

It wasn't until many years later, when I was more or less grown up, that I learned the how and why of Juliet from a woman who had lived in "the Block" with her and knew her story.

Juliet had been born on a farm way out in the country. From the time she was twelve, she had one love and one driving ambition. Her love was horses; her ambition, to become a nurse. Her parents were dirt-poor, but she worked hard, saved whatever money she could earn, and got as much education as came her way.

Then when she was all set to go into training at the hospital, her mother fell ill of consumption. There was no choice. Instead of learning to be a nurse, she had to nurse.

And so the horses won out. They became her only recreation, her salvation. She clipped her hair, wore horsy clothes, rode when she could get hold of a horse, bet when she could lay hands on some extra money, and lived in a man's world in what time she had free from taking care of her mother, who lingered on until Juliet's youth had ended.

And that was the Juliet we'd feared, made fun of, and hated.

Till Someone
Find Us Really Out

That high-school year I won first prize in the Junior Speaking Contest.

My family was jubilant. I wasn't, because I knew I'd won for all the wrong reasons. My piece was a sure-fire laugh-grabber with a song at the end of it — a revolting ditty guaranteed to bring down the house, especially if you couldn't carry a tune, and I couldn't. I'd bellowed my foolishness off-key loud enough to afflict eardrums in the last row of the auditorium. I was a smash hit, but I was a mess inside.

Oh yes, it had taken some "screwing up of courage to the sticking point," as Lady Macbeth said in direr circumstances, to walk out on the stage in full view of the whole village and stand behind the footlights all alone, but it was easier to hide behind the silly stuff I'd been given to elocute than to show real feeling.

And there was the rub. My speech teacher had meant me to do an imaginative poetic play — a dilemma that tore me up inside because to do the poem justice I would have had to let too much of me show. I tried, but I couldn't.

In all my 16 years — or at least all I could remember

— I'd kept myself dammed in, partly because the things I felt were too strong to fit words to, and partly because even if I could express them, I was afraid to let them out. They'd shrivel if they weren't understood.

So I'd settled on the surface for being one of the bunch, fooling around, playing it safe with the slick patter we tossed around to our dates, each other, and anyone else who thrived on the same drivel. It was a way to get along, but I needed more.

The speech teacher was disappointed and out of patience. She said I wasn't trying. I wanted to explain. I couldn't. And while I was making up some watery excuse, I thought of what Robert Frost wrote in "Revelation":

> We make ourselves a place apart
>> Behind light words that tease and flout,
> But oh, the agitated heart
>> Till someone find us really out.

It was lonely and bleak in that "place apart," but my tongue was tied. I'd tied it because I was too unsure of myself to let it speak.

And so the poetic play had gone to a classmate who wasn't one of the bunch — a thin shy girl who hadn't made a dent on anyone's consciousness until she tried out for the speaking contest and won her place with "The Eve of St. Agnes," spoken in a shadowy, unearthly way that set our nerve ends vibrating.

On the night of the contest, she'd spoken her poetic play just before I delivered my silly selection, and I'd wanted to bow out. As far as I was concerned, the contest was over. She had been everything the piece called for. She had shaken me in a wind of feeling.

But I had won the Junior Speaking Contest.

It was a good thing that the prize would not be presented until summer. I don't know how I could have walked up on the stage that evening to receive it. It would have meant passage through fire, and I was already burning with shame and defeat.

Just after school closed in June, I had a telephone call from the principal to tell me that Mrs. J.C. Owens, the summer resident who endowed the prize, wanted to know what book I'd like so that she could order it from the local bookstore.

I told him I wanted *The Oxford Book of English Verse* though I didn't deserve it.

"Oh come now," he said. "Suffering from a bad case of modesty? You won hands down, and don't you forget it. I'll tell Mrs. Owens, and she'll go on from there."

I didn't know what he meant by "go on from there," and I didn't want to know enough to ask him. I was still feeling as cheap and dishonest as I did the night I'd made such a hit in borrowed clothes at the Spring Dance, and I was beginning to wonder whether I'd ever get anywhere as my real self.

A week later I had a note from Mrs. Owens. She had my book and would like me to come to The Crag Tuesday next to receive it. The writing was a shaky copperplate. Very proper, I thought, and old — probably a rickety tartar. And whether she was or wasn't, going to The Crag and talking to her was something I was just plain scared to face.

I had never been in a summer person's house. I had never talked to one of "them." Year-rounders don't except in business dealings. We had been brought up to understand that they were one kettle of fish, we were another, and the two could never mix. Royalty and peasants? Well, not exactly, but the differences were almost as great. Maybe outer-spacers and earthlings was nearer the mark. Anyway, we could be sure of one thing: they never really saw us.

I didn't even know what to wear. Jeans? No. Not proper enough for tea if that's what she had in mind. And the thought of tea was a thought I wished I hadn't thought of. I could hear the china rattling in my shaking hand and see Mrs. Owens looking through me to a time when I wouldn't be there.

But then it was Tuesday, and there was no escape. I

put on my blue denim dress and thong sandals and went forth like a programmed robot.

The Crag was one of the few summer cottages within walking distance of the village. I didn't loiter, but my feet dragged. The nearer I got, the farther away I wished I were. I didn't deserve the prize, but I wanted *The Oxford Book of English Verse*. I was afraid to meet Mrs. Owens, and I was scared to death of tea.

The Crag sat on a height above the sea. Pale pink stucco with dark timbers — not a grand residence as summer cottages go in a wealthy resort but a world away from what I was used to.

It took more courage than I would have believed I had to ring the bell. And before the door opened, I almost ran.

Then a wrinkled gnome of a maid in a black uniform with white pleats across her chest was nodding her head and ushering me in. "Mrs. Owens is expecting you in her study," she said. "Please follow me."

She hippety-hopped up the thickly carpeted stairs, down a long corridor, and into a light-filled room. A lazy fire was mulling away on a small hearth to the right. The windows looked out on a wide expanse of ocean. The furniture was like nothing I'd ever seen — pulled-taffy colored and summer-looking. Books were everywhere on built-in shelves from floor to ceiling, on chairs, piled high on the window seat. And in a straight chair behind a honey-colored desk sat a small woman whose eyes kept flickering and shutting. Mrs. Owens was no rickety tartar. She looked almost as shy as I felt. I suppose the nearest I could come to describing her is to say that she looked like a frightened but intelligent and ready-to-be-friendly monkey.

"Will you sit over there where I can see you?" she said, pointing to a chair away from the light.

I took the chair and waited numbly.

"Why did you ask for *The Oxford Book of English Verse?*" she asked in a kind of faltering voice.

I forgot to be scared. "Because I love poetry," I said.

"Ah, yes," she said almost as if she were talking to herself.

The time had come. I had to tell the truth. "But I don't deserve the prize," I blurted out, my voice coming from down deep inside me. "What I did was nothing — a foolish piece that made people laugh. My classmate did the real speaking with a poetic play I couldn't do and not many people cared enough about to really listen to. She was everything I'd wanted to be and couldn't!"

Mrs. Owens blinked, muttered something I couldn't hear, and picked up her pen. "What I shall write in your book," she said with a sudden glint in her eyes, "is not at all what I had intended to write. You have taken me unawares. I had not expected a fellow-sufferer. Poetry and a feeling of inadequacy. Love and loneliness. Sometime others will understand because they are touched with the same lovely madness — or sanity."

She wrote slowly, almost painfully.

"I shall not keep you here," she said. "You are not comfortable. But read what I have written and go on from there. I know you will." She handed me the book, smiled in a shy, sad way, and said, "Go with the blessing of a friend of poetry."

I said, "Thank you," in a blurred voice, took the book, and left, feeling more upset than ever about why I had won it, but queerly comforted.

When I turned the corner away from the Crag, I looked at what she had written: "This is for a young person who is honest enough to recognize her limitations and who loves the best. She will go far if she keeps on refusing to settle for less. My best wishes, Olivia Owens."

I went home on wings. At last someone had seen me. Mrs. Owens — and she was one of "them" who never looked at us — had looked at me and seen me. Suddenly the world opened up and had no limits. Maybe now, just maybe, I could make it as my real self.

Too Old—Too Young

Jan said we were getting too old. "It's positively infantile," she said in that superior drawl she always puts on shen she was gazing into some invisible mirror and seeing herself as a woman of infinite sophistication.

"You've got to be kidding!" I said. And Lou and Maggie chimed in, muttering and sputtering. "It's the last year we can do it. Who knows where we'll all be next May? And besides, it's . . . it's . . . just plain *fun*." I'd run out of words to say all I meant, and Jan wasn't helping any with that eyebrow up to her hairline.

We'd been hanging around, killing time after school, when the talk had turned to Maybaskets.

It was late April, the ragged edge of winter in Maine. There were still patches of snow where the sun couldn't reach, but pussy willows were swelling and mayflowers were budding in winter-wet leaf beds. In a week it would be Maybasket time.

Our history teacher, who always had some fancy explanation for anything we did, said that hanging Maybaskets was a fertility rite like dancing around a Maypole. We just laughed, thinking of the boys we'd hung to and been hung by ever since we'd been old enough to be let out at night. It was like swapping Valentines or playing Post Office, only more strenuous. The hanger sneaked up to the front door, rang the bell, deposited her paper-filled cone or box full of fudge, jellybeans, or whatever, and then scooted — just fast enough to be caught, roughhoused, and kissed with a resounding smack, or if missed, suffer a head-on collision of noses and teeth. Fertility rite? Well, hardly. The point, besides the fun, was to see how many baskets you'd been hung. We counted them like scalps and publicized the take.

The rules were simple. Girls hung first. Boys chased. Then word got around that it was time to reverse order. The boys' baskets didn't amount to much on the outside — no frills or fringe or scallops for them — but what was inside was something else: real chocolates and plenty of them.

Maybasket night was so many things. The end of winter and slogging around in heavy clothes and boots. A warm stir in the almost-spring air. Thumping hearts, laughter in the dark, creeping and running and tussling. Catching and being caught. We were free things on that night that was like no other in the year.

But now Jan was calling it infantile and saying we were too old because we were seniors in high school. She was going steady with Cal. Mag and I were playing the field, waiting, I guess, for someone who'd make the earth shake under our feet. We felt old and wise when we looked at the funny little freshmen. We felt young and scared when we let ourselves think abut the future and going to college or hunting for a job and being separated.

Maybe we were too old, but we didn't *feel* that way.

"Well, you do what you want," I said, "but I'm hanging Maybaskets."

Mag said, "Me, too."

Lou said, "I've already made some of mine, and I'm not about to waste them."

The walk home was a pretty silent affair. I think we all felt unsettled by this first rift in our group. We couldn't talk about it, but it was there, lying heavy on our minds. It was a relief to get back to where I knew everything would be the same. Mom puttering around the kitchen. Tricks, my cocker, coming at me like a four-legged tornado. My kid brothers hassling each other over whose marbles were whose.

"Had a good day?" Mom asked. She always asked the same question, and I liked it, because no matter whether my day had been good or rotten, I knew she cared. That wouldn't change, at least.

"Oh, okay, except for Jan. She says we're too old for Maybaskets."

Mom stopped doing whatever she was doing at the sink, wiped her hands, and turned around. "Well, are you?" she asked, giving me one of her straight, level looks.

"Guess she's right in a way. It *is* kids' stuff, but I don't *feel* that way!"

"That's good." Mom grinned as if that was exactly what she wanted to hear. Then her face changed, and she had that "I wonder" look that always meant she was nursing some far-out scheme for getting us to do what we wouldn't want to do. "But do you feel *old* enough to hang a basket for me? I've been wracking my brain since Christmas trying to figure out what I could do for Sister Mary Josephine in return for that nice purse she crocheted for me, and I thought if I stuffed some dates and made some of my candied grapefruit peel . . ."

I couldn't believe what I was hearing. Hang a Maybasket to my nun music teacher? Crazy! Worse than crazy. Wild and wrong and impossible! Who ever heard of hanging a Maybasket to a grown-up woman, and a nun at that?

"Mom, you can't mean it! Me sneaking up to the convent, ringing the doorbell at night, waiting for her to come to the door, and . . . oh, Mom, she's *lame*! She can't chase me, and even if she could . . ." The thought of letting her catch me and then . . . My imagination was stretching to what might come then. I shivered.

"Now take it easy. I don't mean for you to hang it and run. Would it be too much to hand her the Maybasket and say, 'My mother and I want you to be part of Maybasket night' ? "

There was no sense arguing. When Mom had set her mind on something, there was no moving her. If I tried, I'd just be proving that I wasn't old enough to handle what seemed sensible enough to Mom.

I was being attacked from both sides. Too old, as Jan saw it. Too young, as Mom saw it.

I wished I'd never heard of Maybaskets.

I didn't tell Mag, Lou, or Jan. Certainly not Jan, who'd give me the full treatment. If she didn't say it, she'd look it — that weary look that meant, "I tried to tell you, but you wouldn't listen." However they'd take it wouldn't — couldn't — change the picture.

We all took piano lessons from Sister Mary Josephine because our parents thought all young ladies should be brought up to play the piano, and Sister Mary Josephine was the only piano teacher in town.

We liked her, if it's all right to say you like a nun. At first we'd been scared to go to the convent. We weren't Catholics so we didn't know what to expect or how to behave. The only Catholic girl we knew was right at home with the nuns. She did a little bob when she met one, said, "Yes, 'ster" and "No, 'ster" as if she was talking to just anyone.

The first time we went was pretty queer. Bare white walls. Silence. A kind of chill as if the windows were always left open to air out whatever life was getting inside. Imagination, of course, but still . . . Then, when Sister Mary Josephine came into the room, her long black habit swirling gracefully around her feet, her rosary jingling a little from the belt around her waist, and we saw that she was pretty and young and smiling we knew it would be all right.

But this business of hanging her a Maybasket was something I *had* to do and hated the thought of doing. What Mom and Sister Mary Josephine didn't know was that I'd been cheating on my lessons. I was never meant to be a musician. I couldn't bear practicing and getting behind or ahead of that perpetual-motion metronome. My only hope was that I might get good enough to play some easy piece that would let me cross my hands and feel like what I guess you'd call a virtuoso. So I'd lied about practicing, and both Mom and Sister Mary Josephine had been taken in by my lies. It was easier with Sister because she liked us to talk a lot, tell her what was going on and how we felt about it. When we'd get round to my playing, I'd say, "I wish I could play this right. I like it, but it's awfully hard." She'd smile a kind of sad smile, play it for me, and say, "That's enough for today," and let me go. I'd feel relieved and dirty at the same time. There was no getting out of it: I *owed* her the Maybasket and whatever else might happen.

The night came too soon for me — all spoiled. The chasing and being chased would have to be put off until I'd got through with Sister Mary Josephine, and by that time the fun would have gone out of it.

The only redeeming feature, if you could call it that, was that Mag and Lou wouldn't have to find out, ever. We were always strictly on our own that night, and I knew that Mom and Sister wouldn't tell — for different reasons.

At 7:30 I marched myself up to the convent door as stiff as if I was on my way to the electric chair. The Maybasket was one of my best creations with soft pink crimped paper in layers around it, a braided pink-and-blue handle, and Mom's special stuff laid out inside on a bed of shredded moss.

I rang the bell and waited numbly. The door opened, and a nun I'd never seen said, "Good evening. May I help you?"

I said fast before my breath gave out, "May I see Sister Mary Josephine?"

She nodded, asked me in, and when I said I'd wait outside, murmured, "As you like. Sister will be with you in a moment."

Again I waited, more alone than I'd ever felt in my life. But one thing was sure: once this was over I was going home and staying there. I didn't want to see another Maybasket as long as I lived.

Then the door opened, and there she was, looking pretty and excited, almost as if she'd been expecting something different and nice to happen.

I made my speech, the one Mom had told me to say, and was turning to go when she said, "Aren't you going to let me chase you?"

I almost dropped dead in my tracks.

"You . . . I . . .?"

"Are you afraid I'll catch you?"

And suddenly I saw how great she was. If I ran full speed, she could never catch me, lame as she was and older and held back by that long full habit. She knew all this, but she still wanted to play.

I put the Maybasket down beside the door and looked her straight in the face for the first time. "Think you can? Come on!"

And I leaped the steps, tore out to the street, and turned to see where she was. Sister Mary Josephine had pulled her habit up to her knees and was running as best she could, unevenly, the lame leg dragging, her face all lighted up with the fun she was having.

I don't know how I knew what to do, but I did it. I started off, stumbled over something that wasn't there, and pulled up short.

She reached me, blowing a little, laughing a lot, and caught me by the arms. "So you let me catch you, didn't you! I knew there was someone under the girl who wouldn't practice and pretended she did. Thank you for *both* Maybaskets." And she took my hand, shook it as if I were a real grown-up, and turned back to the convent.

The rest of the evening was Maybasket night — with a difference. I was not too old; I was not too young; I was just me, knowing something about both, and feeling all put together inside.

The Chicken Dress

I was working summers to help put myself through college, doing whatever came to hand that paid wages. When a new dress shop opened up in my resort village, I applied for the job of salesgirl. One quick sizing up of the owner and his wall-to-wall carpeted boutique was almost enough to send me back to part-time work, but I needed the money so I put on my best face and put out my best sales pitch, and the job was mine, even though I couldn't do alterations.

The owner was a nonstop bustling little man with a deep-piled voice, a heavy foreign accent, and too many "darlings" pronounced "dawling." He was a ball of fire. I wasn't. Our relationship would be something less than a marriage of minds.

The shop was done up in a violent magenta with some kind of gold sparkly stuff in the wall paint. I didn't quite see how it would become me or I it.

"Hours — nine to five. No sitting around between customers. Up on your feet, up on your pretty feet every tick of the clock. You sell, dawling, you sell! These are chicken dresses, the latest dynamite item. Push 'em, sing 'em, sell 'em. That's it. You're hired for a trial week."

In case "chicken dresses" needs some explanation, I can do it fast. These little numbers were flashy, sleazy affairs suited perfectly to aspiring but impecunious Hollywood starlets, of which type we had a sizable dearth wandering around loose in our village. I began to wonder how I was going to "push 'em, sing 'em, sell 'em."

I checked in for work at 8:55 on Monday morning. I stood on my feet. I assumed a posture of purposeful busyness. I studied the price tags. I tried with no success to put breathing room between the cheek-by-jowl dresses. There were too many, and the racks weren't long enough.

No one came in that morning, but still I stood on my feet, my saleslady smile hardened into concrete.

At 11:30 my boss poked his head out of the divided curtain that closed off the stockroom. "Up on your feet? Ready for big business? They'll be coming. You'll see. It's a great little line. They'll eat 'em up."

I was ready to collapse from standing, just standing, when the door opened, and the first potential customer arrived.

She was a heavy woman of about fifty, dressed in a muddled print of no particular shape or style, but it suited her, and she looked right in it. Her best dress, I thought, and now she wants a newer one.

"May I help you?" I said, really wanting to.

"Well, I don't know as you can. I'm a hard one to fit, and I don't do much for my clothes. Still, my man wants me all togged out for the Eden Fair. He's showin' his Rhode Island Reds, and I'm takin' my blackberry jam." She was talking too fast to get it all said before she'd run out of the courage it had taken to get her into this new citified store.

"Let me show you what we have, and we'll see, shall we?" I hoped my voice sounded reassuring enough to pass for the real thing, but I could see no way out of this sickening mess. A chicken dress for this nice country woman?

I riffled through the largest sizes for the least impossible colors and styles. Not much choice, but Push 'em's cold eye was a surgical knife ready to plunge into my back. While she'd been talking, I'd caught a horrid glimpse of his head sticking out between the curtains and his diamond-ringed finger pointing frantically towards the dress racks.

"There now," the woman said as I was hastily sliding by a shocking-pink number with no sleeves and an Empire cut. "My man's forever at me to get something pink. I don't take to it much, but why don't I try it for once? Can't do any harm just to try, can it?"

I extracted the dress from between its too close neighbors, put it over my arm, and took the woman to a dressing room — all this in silence. There was nothing honest I could say without sending my boss into a maniacal rage and hurting the woman badly.

But rage as he would, I refused to hover about while she changed. She had a right to privacy, and she was going to get it.

All too soon the dressing-room door opened, and the woman edged out slowly.

One glance, and I knew what I had to do. The shocking pink had turned her skin a leathery brown. Her bare arms bulged on the outside and sagged on the inside. The straight Empire line rose into a mound over her stomach, pulling the hemline up into a grotesque scallop, and the woman was looking as miserable as I felt.

"I don't know, Miss. I just don't know. It's well enough, but not on me." She needed help. She deserved as gentle truth as I could give her.

"You're absolutely right. It doesn't do a thing for you. I think you'd be much happier in something more like the nice dress you were wearing when you came in." This was a half truth, but it was gentle. "If I were you, I'd take it kind of slow until you find one that feels right on you."

Her eyes brightened. Her mouth pulled up into a steady line, and she looked as if her feet had once again found solid ground to stand on. "I'm obliged to you, Miss. There's not many who wouldn't push." She took my hand in both of hers and shook it up and down.

In five minutes she was gone.

In another five, long enough for the boss to relieve his feelings about college dimwits in general, and me in particular, I was gone, too — back to whatever part-time work I could find, if any.

I should have felt worse than I did. She was a nice woman. I couldn't have done anything else.